GREAT LITTLE DOCTOR

SUSAN LESLIE

Great Little Doctor

The Teaching of
St Thérèse of Lisieux

ST PAULS

By the same author: *The Happiness of God*

ST PAULS Publishing
187 Battersea Bridge Road, London SW11 3AS, UK
www.stpauls.ie

Copyright © ST PAULS 2005

ISBN 085439 712 4

Set by TuKan DTP, Fareham, UK
Printed in Malta by Progress Press Company Limited

ST PAULS is an activity of the priests and brothers
of the Society of St Paul who proclaim the Gospel
through the media of social communication

Contents

Introduction

It seems the fate of St Thérèse of Lisieux to stand at the "wrong end" of Catholicism. Her statue often stands at the rear of a church, or near the side aisles where she stands rather apologetically representing a sickly style of pre-Vatican II piety. This uninspiring image originated partly in the simpering portrait by her sister Céline who surprisingly also took many photographs that present a very different image: a shrewd-looking young woman with a strong face and an expression of steely resolve. Far from being a wilting flower unfit for our times, she appears rather tough. All the same, it is rather unexpected to find her made a Doctor of the Church in 1997.

Susan Leslie has performed a useful service in recasting the image of St Thérèse and indicating in an aptly entitled work why her doctorate is well deserved.

With a wealth of reading and a gimlet eye for detail, Leslie has produced a wise, insightful, well written account with a strong narrative flow. This valuable study gets to the inside of a life, perhaps in the way only a contemplative nun could accomplish. Far from being an escape from the world, enclosed convent life involves a tough confrontation with the limits of the human condition.

Plaster saints appear disembodied and thus, to a degree, inhuman. Leslie is especially good at redressing this notion in relation to St Thérèse who is well displayed here. Spiritually gifted and ambitious for sanctity, she had to practise her heroic virtues in the detail of ordinary life with its ebb and flow, its disappointments and achievements. This study focuses on love, not as something sentimental but a giving that goes against the grain of self-regard. For Thérèse, Christian love emerged from a struggle against the pettiness of some in the convent who treated her badly. Emotionally fragile, Thérèse's battle with herself is well covered in this study; here is no effortless piety of a kind impossible to emulate.

That a sociologist should write this introduction might seem strange. I first met Susan Leslie through her translation of the unfinished doctoral thesis of Marcel Mauss on prayer. Her attention to detail and nuance attracted one's eye. This is an exercise in spiritual biography, not in sociology, yet some wider influences lie behind it that need to be brought out in order to re-set this saint.

Leslie draws out well Thérèse's dark night of the soul when she sat at table with the unbelievers, with the spiritually desolate, experiencing their unbelief with unwavering faith that clung to what she *wanted to believe.*

Here is an uncommonly strongly endowed woman with a spiritual constitution of steel, who will appeal to men and women everywhere.

The times are dim, hope is feeble, trust is low and the future looks bleak. Leslie stresses the solidarity Thérèse offers in these troubled times, where the baleful legacy of Nietzsche still lingers. Thérèse has made this journey ahead of these times and from her life there is much to be mined. After her death, Thérèse's powers of intercession became legendary, especially for the French soldiers of the First World War and for struggling priests and missionaries.

This is an unexpectedly gripping and accessible account that well conveys the making of a saint well fitted for our times. Insightful and economically written, this is a highly readable study that will last. There is much to be learnt from it, not least the practical facets of St Thérèse's theology that were forged in the ordinary. It shows why St Thérèse well deserves the title of doctor and why she should be re-set at the "right end" of Catholicism. Certainly, after reading this study, one will light a candle before her statue to help to see the better in the dark episodes of life. Moving her up the side aisles would help light another candle on another occasion.

Dr Kieran Flanagan
Reader in Sociology, University of Bristol

1
Little Doctor

Thérèse is a ruse of the Holy Spirit.

Emmanuel Mounier

There is silence in the catechism class at the Benedictine school of Lisieux. Young brows are furrowed, searching in vain for the answer to the Abbé Domin's question. "Come now," urges the priest, "Jeanne? Félicie? Louise?"

The girls continue to frown but no answer is forthcoming. Then the youngest leaps to her feet and recites the answer faultlessly. The older girls are discomfited while young Thérèse Martin basks in her moment of glory.

"Well done, Thérèse!" applauds the Abbé. "Don't I always call you my little doctor?"

Some hundred and fifteen years later, this same child was to be declared a doctor of the Church. Thérèse and her family would have laughed at the very idea; the Abbé would probably have had apoplexy.

Today there are many people who express shock and disapproval that the child of Lisieux (the *Little Flower*!) should have been admitted to the august company of female doctors of the Church. For Thérèse is only the third woman to have been so honoured and her companions, Catherine of Siena in the fourteenth century and Teresa in the sixteenth, seem at first sight to outclass Thérèse by a very long way. Catherine and Teresa are, by any reckoning, spiritual giants. The briefest glance at their stories will confirm this.

Catherine, the most plebeian of our three saints, was the youngest of the twenty-five children born to Giacomo Benincasa, a Sienese dyer, and his wife Mona. Catherine had her first mystical experience at the age of six, steadfastly refused to marry and became a Dominican tertiary while a young woman. After many years spent in a cell within her family home, she emerged from her solitude to nurse the sick in the hospitals of Siena and later gathered around her a group of disciples: old and young, religious, priests and lay people, poets and politicians. What attracted these people? Evidently it was Catherine's radiant holiness, her exuberant love for God and the Church, her disposition which was at once tender towards the weak and sinful and inflexible in the demands she made on her followers. They called her Mama although she was younger than them all; they bowed to her wisdom although she had no formal education.

Soon the sphere of Catherine's influence extended to popes, princes and warring political parties. Her four hundred extant letters, addressed to churchmen, governors, nuns, prisoners and prostitutes, show her as bold, affectionate and persuasive by turns. Amidst all this activity, Catherine's prayer continued to be intense, often ecstatic. She experienced the phenomenon of mystical death, she received the stigmata. It was out of her prayer that her books emerged. Her first biographer, Raymond of Capua, explains, "Such clarity of truth was revealed to her from heaven that Catherine was constrained to spread it abroad by means of writing." In her Dialogue and Treatise of Divine Providence, she sets forth her teaching in the vernacular of her own Sienese dialect. Hers is no new doctrine but she brings to the traditional wisdom of the Church an astonishing freshness and vitality. There is a strong sense of urgency in these lines from the opening of the Dialogue,

"A soul rises up, restless with tremendous desire for God's honour and the salvation of souls… And loving she seeks to pursue truth and clothe herself in it." These words could well serve as her epitaph.

Towards the end of her life, exhausted as she was by

her efforts at political and ecclesiastical reconciliation, she had a vision of her heart being pressed out as balm over the Church. Her influence over her contemporaries was considerable but necessarily transitory; the balm of her dedicated life still spreads fragrance in the Church she loved so well.

Whereas Catherine of Siena seems to have been holy almost from the cradle, Teresa of Avila was one of God's reluctant saints. Her early life in an aristocratic Castilian family was marked more by frivolity than by religious fervour. She was fond of novels, dancing and fine clothes. She admits that she entered the Carmelite convent in Avila at the age of twenty, not because she wished to become a nun but because she feared marriage. There were no other real options for a well-born woman of her time. The Convent of the Incarnation in Avila was extremely lax, almost a residential club for pious ladies. The nuns gave concerts and parties and entertained their friends and admirers in the parlour. Jewellery was worn over the austere Carmelite habit, monastic fare enlivened by gifts of rich food from relatives. Strict enclosure was not observed.

After spending some twenty years under this relaxed regime, Teresa underwent a true conversion. She began to pray in earnest and to experience visions, ecstasies and interior voices. Sometimes, to her considerable embarrassment, she levitated in church. Her best-known vision, immortalised by Bernini's statue, the Ecstasy of St Teresa, is the transverberation where an angel pierced her heart with a burning lance. Teresa was always cautious in attaching importance, let alone merit, to such manifestations. Sanctity, she taught, was a matter of loving God and doing his will, not of seeing visions and dreaming dreams.

As Teresa's prayer deepened, so did her dissatisfaction with her lax form of monastic life. So it was in 1562 that she founded the small, extremely poor convent of St Joseph at Avila. Many other houses were to follow and in the late

1560's she helped St John of the Cross to carry out a similar reform among the Carmelite friars. The reform of both nuns and friars was carried out in the teeth of fierce opposition both from the Carmelite order and the ecclesiastical authorities. The papal nuncio called Teresa "an unquiet gadabout, a disobedient and quarrelsome woman", adding the unfortunate words, "and she teaches theology as though she were a doctor of the Church!" Like Catherine, Teresa drew her theological teaching from her own experience of God. For her nuns she wrote *The Way of Perfection*, about prayer and the practice of the Christian life. A later work, *The Interior Castle*, describes the soul's journey to God and is usually regarded as her most mature account of prayer and contemplation. The Foundations is a lively description of the sixteen reformed houses that she established in Spain. She also wrote her autobiography that contains valuable expositions of the life of prayer.

It is hardly surprising that Teresa attracted the attention of the Inquisition. Was she teaching error? Were her views on prayer tainted by the doctrines of the *alumbrados,* a sect that had already fallen foul of the religious authorities?

"God knows with what sincerity I have written what is true," protested Teresa but added, "I submit myself to the correction of the Church." Teresa's writings were examined and found to be sound; over the centuries they have enlightened countless men and women of all denominations and none.

In spite of her raptures, ecstasies and levitations, Teresa is usually remembered as a down-to-earth saint, a hugely practical mystic, full of good humour and common sense. To those who strive too earnestly for an angelic life she says robustly:

> "We are not angels. We have bodies. To want to be angels here on earth is absurd – particularly if you are as much part of the earth as I am."

Now we come to Thérèse of Lisieux, the shortest-lived of our three saints. Catherine died at the age of thirty-three, Teresa at sixty-seven, Thérèse at a mere twenty-four. As Thérèse lay mortally ill, one of the other nuns was heard wondering what the prioress would find to say about Sr Thérèse of the Child Jesus when she died. Thérèse was gentle and virtuous but there wasn't much else to say about her... Fortunately the prioress had to hand a ready-made "death notice" in the form of Thérèse's autobiography, *The Story of a Soul*, which the young nun had written at the request of her former superior who was also her blood sister, Pauline. Thérèse had set to work, balancing a school exercise book on her knees; and that is how, eventually, her story spread throughout the world.

It is not strictly accurate to say that Thérèse's life was uneventful but it was certainly played out in a lower key than those of her two sister doctors of the Church. Catherine and Teresa were well known in their lifetime. Catherine, with her family of disciples, her battles on behalf of popes, her ecclesiastical and political influence, was once described as "the most famous woman in Christendom". Teresa undertook the reform of Carmel and was respected during her lifetime as a mistress of the spiritual life. Thérèse, on the other hand, created little stir during her short life yet her story, published a year after her death, proved curiously compelling. The autobiography passed from hand to hand; it was reprinted and translated. The author was to become, in the words of Pope Pius IX, "the greatest saint of modern times". So perhaps we should take a closer look at a life that has inspired and continues to inspire countless other lives. Maybe there is more to Thérèse than meets the eye.

Thérèse was born in 1873 in the Norman town of Alençon. She was the youngest of the nine children born to Louis and Zélie Martin. Two boys and a girl had died in infancy; Thérèse was the last of the surviving girls. The

Martins belonged to the *petite bourgeoisie*; Louis was a watchmaker and jeweller, Zélie was skilled in the making of fine lace, the famous *point d'Alençon*. Theirs was a devout household; both parents attended daily Mass and the children were carefully instructed in the faith. Zélie's sister Marie-Louise was a nun at the Visitation convent of le Mans. The consecrated state was held in honour in the family – both Louis and Zélie had at one time wanted to embrace the religious life – but there was fun as well as fervour in the Martin home: picnics and excursions and social gatherings at the local *cercle catholique.*

Aunt Marie-Louise disapproved of this last "frivolity" but Madame Martin briskly defended her daughter's right to wholesome recreation: "We can go along with some of the things the holy daughter says but not all of them; we can't live like wolves after all!"

Thérèse's first four-and-a-half years were happy ones. She recalled later that everything on earth had smiled at her. And she smiled back, a lively, intelligent infant, the darling baby of the family.

In August 1877, Zélie Martin died of breast cancer. Thérèse was deeply affected and became suddenly shy and withdrawn and tiresomely tearful for years afterwards. The family moved to Lisieux to be near Zélie's brother Isodore, his gentle wife Céline and their daughters Jeanne and Marie. Pauline and Marie Martin undertook the care of Thérèse and it was largely thanks to their loving but firm upbringing that she escaped being spoilt. Louis tended to indulge his "little queen" who was showered with gifts and generally cosseted by Papa. There was one occasion, however, on which the whole Martin family united to protect young Thérèse's interests. Thérèse refers to it in her autobiography, saying that when the first communion children made their act of dedication to the Blessed Virgin Mary, it was only fitting that the motherless Thérèse should speak the words of the prayer. In fact another child had been chosen and it was only through the concerted Martin family machinations that the honour was finally accorded to Thérèse.

In stark contrast to the loving warmth of Thérèse's family home, les Buissonnets, was her school, the Benedictine Abbey of Lisieux. Thérèse hated it: "the unhappiest days of my life". She spent only five years there and completed her studies with a private tutor in the town.

When Thérèse was nine, Pauline, the second eldest Martin girl, entered the Carmel of Lisieux. Thérèse was devastated. Pauline had been a second mother to her since Zélie's death; now she was bereaved afresh. Five months later, Thérèse suffered a violent attack of chorea, possibly precipitated by her grief over Pauline and by an ill-timed conversation with Uncle Isodore about her dead mother. Thérèse grew delirious and the family feared, first for her reason, then for her life. During the worst episode of her illness, Thérèse and her sisters Marie, Léonie and Céline begged the Blessed Virgin's aid. Suddenly, as Thérèse gazed at the statue of Mary that stood at her bedside, she saw the Virgin smiling at her and knew that her prayer had been answered; she was cured.

"She was beautiful and she smiled at me," Thérèse explained reluctantly when Marie demanded to know the cause of the sudden change in the invalid. Marie naturally wanted to tell the Carmelites and on Thérèse's next visit to the convent parlour, she was confronted by excited nuns requesting an exact account of the miracle. But there was no more to say: the Virgin had been beautiful and she had smiled. The good nuns were disappointed at this unadorned recital and a bewildered Thérèse began to wonder if the whole affair, illness and miraculous cure, had been mere illusion.

Thérèse's first communion, a year later, coincided with Pauline's Carmelite vows. Marie also entered Carmel in 1886. Léonie entered a Poor Clare convent at about this time but her poor health forced her to return home after only three months; considerably later she was to become a nun of the Visitation in Caen.

Thérèse longed for Carmel but as she frankly admits in her autobiography she seemed scarcely fitted for such an austere life. Her health was delicate, her sensibilities even more so. She wept about anything and everything and expected appreciation and thanks for the least good deed. Her forthright sister Céline, looking back on this period of Thérèse's life and speaking unusually euphemistically, says, "It was as if God had cast a veil over her good qualities." Thérèse's self-assessment is blunter: "I was really unbearable!"

Happily for Thérèse and her long-suffering family, she was fast approaching what she calls her "complete conversion", the time when she was to regain the robust character she had lost at her mother's death. It happened overnight. The old Thérèse left for midnight Mass on Christmas eve in 1886 and in the small hours of the next day a new Thérèse was born: unselfish, courageous and incredibly ambitious. Gone were the tears and emotional demands; now all she wanted was to become a saint. And she knew even then the price of sanctity: much suffering, a constant striving for perfection, utter forgetfulness of self.

The following May, Thérèse begged her father's permission to enter Carmel at the age of fifteen. Louis reluctantly consented but he was the only one to do so. Uncle Isodore opposed the idea, as did the local bishop and the chaplain of Carmel. Even Pauline was unenthusiastic at first. Louis created a diversion by taking Céline and Thérèse on a pilgrimage to Rome. "I shall ask the Pope", decided Thérèse who naively imagined that the Holy Father would recognise the genuineness of her vocation and instantly grant her request. Instead, he gently advised her to leave the matter to her superiors. Not many months later, rather surprisingly, permission was granted; Thérèse was to enter Carmel on 9 April 1888. She was fifteen years and three months old.

Thérèse spent only nine years in Carmel. Although she was in good health when she entered, she tells us that she had always felt that her earthly life would be short. Maybe that is why she speaks of "hurrying along the way of love". She certainly gives the impression of one who wanted to waste no time. Her ambition remained lofty: "I want to love God as much as our holy Mother St Teresa," the novice informed an astonished and disapproving confessor.

"I want to be a great saint," announced the ambitious Thérèse. Yet the realistic Thérèse had to admit that the great saints loomed above her like mountain peaks while she was a mere grain of sand. How was she to become a saint at all? Looking back at her childhood, she recalled an amusing episode that seemed to throw light on the problem.

Léonie, deeming herself too old to play with dolls, had offered her younger sisters the choice of a basketful of dolls' clothes and pretty scraps of material. Céline selected a packet of braid but Thérèse announced, "I choose everything!" and marched off with the whole basket. Later, she says, when presented with the idea of perfection, she chose everything that God willed. Perfection, she realised, consisted in doing God's will, being what he wanted one to be. Evidently God did not want Thérèse to be a saint in the grand manner; visions, ecstasies, raptures, all the outward signs popularly associated with sanctity, were not for her. She could not even manage bodily penance; the one penitential instrument she tried, a spiked bracelet, gave her a septic sore and had to be discarded. No, Thérèse was to find holiness in small things, in the mosaic of little virtues that would make up her Little Way to God.

By January 1896, Thérèse had completed the main body of her manuscript that was to be published after her death as *The Story of a Soul*. In the April of that same year, she began to spit blood, the first sign of the pulmonary tuberculosis that was to kill her. Thérèse, far from being alarmed, was overjoyed at the thought of going to heaven. She simply could not understand how anyone could lack faith. And then she suddenly understood only too well; her radiant assurance of heaven abruptly disappeared and she had to cling to God in almost total darkness. Her faith never deserted her but the radiance was gone forever. Until her death the following year, she received only lightning flashes of consolation and, as she sadly remarks, these flashes made the surrounding night seem darker still.

In agony of body and soul, Thérèse made her final journey to God. Already her sisters were beginning to discern her holiness. They rather unnervingly sat at her bedside making notes of her conversations; they asked her to add explanatory chapters to her autobiography. They sought her counsel and laughed at her jokes that included some truly dreadful puns. When the convent chaplain asked her if she was resigned to death, she exclaimed, "Oh father, it's *life* I need to be resigned to!" But she trusted that the God who had never failed her would sustain her to the end. "I don't regret having given myself to Love!" whispered Thérèse as she lay dying. And when the final moment came, she summed up in a sentence the whole of her brief life: "Oh I love him... my God, I... love... you!"

As she neared death, Thérèse had expressed a wish to tell many others of God's goodness, mercy and love. She wanted, she said, to spend her heaven doing good on earth. She wished to propagate her "little doctrine", her Little Way of holiness so that a "multitude of little souls" might follow in her wake. Her wishes were granted. The first edition of her autobiography, published in 1898, was swiftly sold out. The Carmel was inundated with requests for the book, for further information about Thérèse, even for relics. Eventually *The Story of a Soul* was translated into more than fifty languages and people all over the world attributed miracles to Thérèse's intercession. Enthusiastic testimonials swelled the convent's mailbag; there were hundreds, then thousands of letters. Thérèse's cause was opened in 1909 and she was canonised in 1925, just twenty-five years after her death. In 1997 she was made a doctor of the Church.

Thérèse was very young and apparently very ordinary. What, we may wonder, does she have in common with the ardent Catherine, the brilliant Teresa? She was, like them, both reformer and teacher. Whereas Catherine was concerned with the reform of Church and papacy and Teresa with that of the Carmelite Order, Thérèse's main interest was the reform of individual souls. She believed that if only "little souls", that is, the vast majority, could understand the depths of God's tenderness, none would fail to scale the mountain of Love. Thérèse is counted as a doctor of the Church because, like Catherine and Teresa, not only did she live her faith with heroic enthusiasm but she also left a body of teaching. She called it her "little doctrine", her Little Way to God.

Let us not be deceived by that recurring "little"; it hides a heroic way of holiness, simple but stark. Let us not be deluded by Thérèse's smiling face nor distracted by the sugary piety associated with her cult. Thérèse is no simpering infant but a great little doctor. As Chesterton so sapiently remarked, this saint is indeed a little flower – made of wrought iron. Yet many still ask, "Can any good come out of Lisieux?" Come and see.

2

Herald of Mercy

> My merciful God comes to meet me.
>
> *Psalms*
>
> As a grain of sand weighs less than gold, so the demand for just judgment weighs less with God than his compassion.
>
> *Isaac of Syria, seventh century*

Thérèse bends over her exercise book at the Abbey School. Grammar! Not her favourite subject. She has embellished the page with a wobbly line of leaves, blotched flowers, a cross, a Sacred Heart, some doodles that could be feathers. Ah well, down to work – Analyse the following: "Children who are obedient are loved by the good God."

This is probably typical of the exercises set by the good nuns: grammar with a message! Thérèse had imbibed this particular message with her mother's milk. As a tiny child, she was constantly seeking reassurance: "Have I been good today?" For she knew that only the good were pleasing to God, only the faithful would eventually go to heaven. As for the others, well, they would be damned; any Catholic child knew that. But it bothered Thérèse and after a school doctrine class on salvation and damnation, she was heard to remark, "I think if I were the good God I would save them *all*!"

From earliest childhood, Thérèse questioned religious attitudes and customs. She seemed to compare what she was taught with her own inner vision of God. Her particular genius lay in her ability to translate that vision into teaching that spoke to ordinary people of the love and mercy of God. Thérèse is a little doctor because she is simple and speaks to the simplest souls; she is great in that she helped the whole Church to rediscover the God of tenderness and compassion.

The great doctors of old – a Gregory, an Ambrose, an Augustine, a Jerome – battled with major heresies and in the process hammered out the great doctrines of faith. Thérèse, on a much humbler scale, fought against the minor heresies that make God too small, too mean.

Thérèse had discovered in her own life a God whose mercy outran his justice, a God who counts our love and not the number of our pious acts, a God who is to be sought, not on the high mountains of endeavour but in the lowly valley of humility.

"No, no, no, you're going the wrong way!" she would admonish the novices entrusted to her care and then she would lead them firmly from the partial truths of heresy to the fullness of faith.

The minor heresies demolished by Thérèse are perhaps the more pernicious for being little; they pass unnoticed because they are not dramatic distortions of truth but merely an incomplete picture of the love of God. Thérèse was concerned to show that we can never have too much confidence in God; he is so mighty, so merciful.

It was because Thérèse was so deeply conscious of God's mercy that she questioned the black-and-white view of Christian life.

Now black-and-whiteness is a necessary starting-point for children. Therein lies the great value of the fairytale; the bad are very bad and come to a sticky end whereas the good are very good and live happily ever after. This is excellent for the tinies but quite inadequate for adults. Yet Thérèse and her contemporaries were taught a black-and-white version of religion: God rewards good and punishes evil. There is no peace for the wicked – and little peace for the righteous either, with a fault-finding God forever peering over their shoulders. No wonder scruples flourished in such an atmosphere.

The road to heaven was presented, not as the gracious highway of Isaiah, "in which even fools do not stray" but as a path strewn with the most appalling obstacles. The preacher at Thérèse's retreat for her second communion filled the children with terror when he spoke to them of mortal sin.

Mortal sin certainly exists but alongside it is the infinite mercy of God. The justice of God certainly exists but Thérèse saw it as a *reason for his mercy*. Seeing human weakness, she reasoned, his justice obliges him to take that weakness into account. She could never understand how anyone could be afraid of such a tender friend.

Thérèse became a champion of the mercy of God partly as a result of her pondering of the Scriptures, partly through her own experience of God's tenderness. Thérèse loved the stories of the Prodigal Son, the Labourers in the Vineyard, the Good Thief. They had all found salvation, not because they were good but because God is merciful.

At first sight, it seems strange that Thérèse, who, according to one of her confessors had never committed a mortal sin, should have so vigorously taken the part of sinners. In fact she had a unique way of regarding her own comparative sinlessness: God had forgiven her in advance by preventing her from sinning seriously. Thérèse had heard that pure souls did not love God as ardently as repentant sinners. Mary Magdalene was often cited as an example of this: she loved much because she was forgiven much. How Thérèse would have liked to prove them wrong! To illustrate her point, she told one of the delightful parables which enliven her writings: a doctor's son stumbles over a great stone, injures himself and is grateful to be healed by his father. But supposing the father had run ahead and removed the stone so that the son could not injure himself; wouldn't the son be even more grateful? Thérèse evidently thought so.

Thérèse had received dramatic proof of God's mercy to an apparently hardened sinner. It was at the outcome of a *cause célèbre* that shook the whole of France during Thérèse's adolescence. Henri Pranzini had murdered three women in a Paris apartment. Condemned to death, he denied his guilt and repulsed the ministrations of the prison chaplain. Meanwhile, Thérèse was praying fervently for Pranzini. She knew that God was merciful but just for her consolation, she asked for a sign of the prisoner's repentance. On the morning of his execution, Pranzini's head was already in place beneath the guillotine when the condemned man suddenly summoned the chaplain and kissed the proffered crucifix three times. Thérèse had her sign and she was always to think of Pranzini as her "first child"; the God of mercy had heard her prayers; doubtless Pranzini would follow the Good Thief into paradise.

Thérèse constantly rejected the Jansenist rigorism that still lingered in the Church of her day. She was not in the least attracted to the then fashionable offering of oneself to divine justice. This was an offering made by heroic souls who consented to suffer the rigours of God's wrath, so diverting that wrath from the sinners who had deserved it. Thérèse proposed another sort of heroism: she would offer herself to be a victim of the divine mercy. God's heart, she explained, was full of a love that longed to flow into human hearts, many of which ignored or rejected that love. Thérèse offered herself as a receptacle of God's infinite tenderness; she would allow God's love to flow through her, to consume her in its fire.

Thérèse uses the expressions "victim", "holocaust" and "martyrdom of love" but her aim is love, not suffering. If we give ourselves to be vessels of God's love, we shall certainly suffer. Therèse warned that one must expect to be sacrificed without reserve. Imagine what she is asking: that the fire of God's love should invade her heart. Naturally that heart will be burnt as well as warmed for, in this world, love and suffering go hand in hand. But the emphasis is on sacrifice in the true sense of "making holy", not on the suffering involved.

Thérèse encouraged her sister Céline and one of her novices to make the Offering to Merciful Love. However, her elder sister Marie was reluctant to join them; she didn't want to suffer any more! Thérèse reassured her that she had nothing to fear: from God's love we could only obtain mercy.

Marie was not alone in misunderstanding Thérèse's Offering of Myself as a Victim of Holocaust to God's Merciful Love. To many people the word "victim" immediately suggests suffering. Thus when Thérèse was canonised, the lesson for her feast day originally read, "Inflamed with a *desire to suffer*, she offered herself as a victim to the merciful love of God." Mother Agnes of Jesus, Thérèse's sister Pauline, insisted on a change: "Inflamed with *holy charity*." "If they can so deform Thérèse's thought during our lifetime, what will it be like after our death?" asked the prioress.

To Thérèse, becoming a victim of God's mercy meant to live in one single act of perfect love. Now this single act is necessarily composed of a multitude of separate acts but the eyes of the soul should be fixed on God, not on the acts themselves. Yet it is all too easy to concentrate on counting acts of love and so to make religion a branch of mathematics – higher, of course!

Thérèse's contemporaries were decidedly mathematical in their approach to God: so many Hail Mary's, so many pious aspirations, so many acts of penance. Sound familiar? We could call it the "accountant mentality" and it is still with us, though perhaps to a lesser extent than in Thérèse's day.

The child Thérèse was an enthusiastic religious

accountant, beginning at the age of three with a "rosary of practices". This was a string of movable beads; each time the owner made a "sacrifice", one bead was moved along the string: an extremely self-conscious method of practising virtue! And when Thérèse was preparing for her first communion, her sister Pauline made her a little book in which to record her prayers, penances and various acts of virtue, all of which were represented by flowers. Thérèse clocked up eight hundred and eighteen sacrifices and two thousand seven hundred and seventy-three acts or aspirations of love. This was the style of the day and doubtless encouraged prayerfulness and devotion.

Later on, Thérèse came to understand that to become a saint, one must suffer much, always seek the most perfect thing and *forget oneself.* The penance and the search for perfection are still there but without the self-preoccupation that is the enemy of true holiness. Jesus was teaching her not to count her acts but to do everything out of love.

According to Thérèse, Jesus has only one defect: he can't count! Thérèse explains that when a great sinner turns to God at the last minute, God does not calculate all the graces wasted, all the sins committed; he counts only the last prayer and receives the penitent soul immediately into the arms of his mercy.

One good reason for us not to calculate our acts of virtue, is that everything we do for God pales into insignificance beside all that he has done for us. Our love is so easily tainted with self-seeking or self-congratulation. Isaiah states unequivocally "All our righteousness is filthy rags." Yet it is easy to feel complacent when we have "done something for God". Thérèse's sister Céline, who was also her novice in Carmel, fell into this trap. Céline had turned down an advantageous marriage and had renounced an artistic career in order to become a nun and she asked Thérèse to write a poem reminding Jesus of these noble sacrifices. The refrain, Céline stipulated, was to be

"Remember!" Thérèse accepted the commission and produced a long poem reminding Céline of all that Jesus had done for her; there was no mention at all of the heroic novice. It was a salutary lesson but a gentle one; the poem is very beautiful and Céline was to treasure it.

Again and again Thérèse returns to the themes of God's mercy and love: a merciful love that stoops to conquer even the least of his erring children, a love that is satisfied only when it has abased itself to our nothingness in order to turn that nothingness into fire. It was this fiery love that made saints.

Sanctity! That had been Thérèse's ambition since her early teens. She felt that she was born for glory but God had made her understand that her glory would not be evident to mortal eyes, that it would consist in becoming a great saint.

The only problem with this goal was that it was unattainable. The great saints still towered above her like mountain peaks; she was still just a very small grain of sand in the valley below. Gradually she realised that the grain of sand was never going to grow into a mountain. Little souls were little souls and evermore would be so. Somehow she had to find a way to holiness that was possible to ordinary people like her.

Thérèse came to believe that sanctity was itself an expression of God's mercy. It was a merciful Creator who had bestowed perfection not only on fragrant roses and magnificent lilies but also on humble violets and simple daisies. One need not be a saint after the grand manner but one could still be a saint, even a great saint, in a small way. This was the paradox that ran through the Scriptures; God often chose the weak, the poor, the insignificant. There was David, the youngest son tending the sheep, Gideon the least of his family in the least important tribe, Moses the poor speaker, Isaiah who was only a youth. And had not the greatest saint of all declared, "He has exalted those of low

26

degree, he has filled the hungry with good things."? One did not even need a natural aptitude for holiness as this text, dear to Thérèse, bears witness,

"There is another who is slow and needs help, lacking ability and full of poverty, yet the eye of the Lord has looked on him for good and has lifted him up from his low estate and has exalted his head, and many have wondered at him and glorified God."[1]

Slow, needing help, lacking ability and full of poverty: that is a perfect description of Thérèse's "little soul".

Thérèse had originally dreamt, no doubt, of being a great soul. After her "complete conversion" at the age of thirteen, she tells us that she made "giant strides" in the way of perfection. She battled her way into Carmel at the age of fifteen, determined to give every ounce of her love to Jesus. She would conquer holiness at the point of the sword... Yet somehow it didn't happen that way. The child who had mused with her sister Céline on the beauties of heaven, is now reduced to daily aridity in prayer. She cannot talk about her soul to her novice mistress; the prioress constantly finds fault with her. Papa's little queen has become, in the eyes of her less charitable companions, "the big kid". It is difficult not to be disheartened.

But Thérèse had resolved at her first communion never to be discouraged. She thinks back to her infancy and recalls another potentially discouraging situation: trying to climb the stairs in her Alençon home. One can still see the stairs that the infant Thérèse failed to climb; they are steep and deep. "Maman! Maman!" called Thérèse at each unsuccessful attempt. Finally her mother took pity on her feeble child and carried her to the top.

As an adult, Thérèse came to feel that she was too small to climb the steep stairway of perfection, but God, whose heart is more tender than that of any mother, would take pity on her and lift her up. Yet the infant must keep on trying to climb. Not until we have done our feeble best will

God intervene. The infant is weak but it must persevere. Weakness and perseverance, humble trust in God's merciful love, these are the characteristics of Thérèse's alternative route up the steep stairway of perfection, a route she was to call the Little Way.

3

A Little Way to Heaven

Beware of posing as a profound person;
God became a baby.

Oswald Chambers

O Jesus, how little we understand the mystery of
sanctification! We think that we personally have such a large
part to play. Alas, our sole contribution is to acknowledge
our perpetual inconstancy, never growing tired of our
repeated failures. The rest is your work.

R.P. Schryvers, CSSP – **The Gift of Self**

All efforts at do-it-yourself sanctity end in one of two cul-
de-sacs: discouragement or dishonesty. We either lay down
our arms in despair or we pretend to ourselves and others
that we are indeed going forward under our own steam.
This means that we have failed to understand the basic
biblical truths expressed in Jesus' "Without me you can
do nothing" and Paul's "By grace you are saved."

Thérèse's fundamental honesty prevented her from
pretending to a sanctity she did not possess. She had tried
very hard, it is true, but she was far from being a perfect
nun. She couldn't even keep awake at her prayers! She had
critical thoughts about her Sisters and when tempted to
answer back or justify herself, she had to take to flight;
otherwise, she admits she would not have been strong
enough to hold her tongue. She was a willing worker but
clumsy and slow; the baby of the Buissonnets was not used
to housework. These were small faults but they were faults
all the same and she so longed for perfection. "Be perfect
as your heavenly father is perfect." Christ's words echoed
in her heart. How far she was from that!

But perfection must be possible, reasoned Thérèse; otherwise Christ would not have commanded it. Also, she had been convinced for years that she was called to be a great saint. And St John of the Cross assured her that God never inspires desires which he does not mean to satisfy.

Thérèse was back in Alençon, an infant trying in vain to climb those steep stairs. Maybe, she thought, there was some way round the problem, a short cut. Then she remembered how, on her visits to Italian hotels, she had seen for the first time the marvellous new invention called a lift. All she needed was to find a spiritual lift! She set herself to pray and search the Scriptures.

Prayer was straightforward enough; searching the Scriptures was another matter. In Thérèse's day, Catholics did not have access to the Bible in its entirety. There were the lessons read at Mass and divine office and other selected passages. Thérèse had the Gospels but she never possessed the whole Bible that we today take for granted. However, when Céline entered Carmel in 1894, she brought with her several exercise books full of biblical quotations. Thérèse pounced on these with delight and found the "lift" she was seeking. First came these words from Proverbs:

"If anyone is very small let them come to me."[1]

Later on, Thérèse came upon this:

"As a mother comforts her child, so I will comfort you; I will carry you on my bosom and dandle you on my knees."[2]

Thérèse concluded that the lift that would carry her to heaven was the arms of Jesus. She did not need to grow; on the contrary, she must stay small and become even smaller. In that way she could be sure that Jesus would carry her in his arms.

At first sight this seems a strange ambition. At the time of Thérèse's Christmas conversion, had she not rejoiced to be freed from the swaddling clothes of infancy? Why this sudden desire to retrace her steps? What possible connection could there be between infantile regression and sanctity? It is indeed puzzling until we look more closely at Thérèse's conversion, an event that in retrospect can be seen as the very beginning of the Little Way.

It was Christmas morning in the year 1886. Monsieur Martin, Céline and Thérèse had just returned from midnight Mass. According to French custom, children were given small gifts placed in shoes on the hearth. Thérèse, nearly fourteen, should have outgrown such childishness but Céline had prepared the "enchanted shoes" all the same; after all, Thérèse *was* the baby of the family. Monsieur Martin, however, was weary and burst out irritably, "Thank goodness it's the last year of this!" From the landing, Thérèse overheard the remark and her eyes filled with tears. "Don't go down yet!" whispered Céline but Thérèse was already half way to the parlour where, laughing merrily, she opened her gifts while her sister blinked in amazement and Papa, quite recovered, joined in the fun.

Suddenly, recalls Thérèse, her heart was filled with charity, making her forget herself in order to please others... God had to work a small miracle to make her grow up in an instant.

Was it such a small miracle? Perhaps not, when one considers how difficult it is to change gear emotionally. And for Thérèse it was not merely a change of gear; it was more like a U-turn.

The history of spirituality is full of such U-turns. Sometimes the occasion is dramatic: the Good Thief discerns in Christ crucified the Lord of paradise; Saul of Tarsus is struck to the ground on the Damascus road; the Irish highwayman repents as he falls dying from his horse. But there is another kind of conversion, which, like that of Thérèse, is occasioned by an apparently trivial event. Let us take just two examples: St Augustine in the sixth century

31

and Br Lawrence in the sixteenth. St Augustine's conversion dated from the moment when he heard a child's voice piping, "Take and read! Take and read!" Augustine took and read the Scripture passage that was to change his life, a life that was to influence Western Christendom for centuries thereafter. As for Br Lawrence, he was converted by a tree! The sight of a tree in spring leaf so filled him with wonder at God's goodness that he became a Carmelite lay brother and wrote the spiritual classic The Practice of the Presence of God.

Saint Augustine and Br Lawrence both turned from worldly pursuits to the love of God. Thérèse, like all her family, could hardly have been called worldly. The Martins were not just outwardly devout; they lived their religion from morning to night. Thérèse's day began with her sister Pauline's question, "Have you given your heart to God?" and every evening the child would anxiously ask if she had been pleasing to God. In such an atmosphere the word "conversion" is somewhat surprising. But if we look more closely, we shall see its appropriateness.

Thérèse's childhood had been dogged by hyper-sensitivity, scruples and painful self-absorption. Until her conversion, she had earnestly striven to love and serve God but she had, as it were, been facing in the wrong direction. She had been watching herself, anxiously counting both her sins and her sacrifices. Then, at the end of her thirteenth year, she turned round to face God. She had just received in Holy Communion the strength and power of God and it was he who, taking pity on her thitherto-fruitless efforts at self-conquest, became himself her strength. Like the mother at the top of the staircase, God came down and lifted his child to a higher level. Thérèse knew that, left to herself, she would not have been able to force back her self-piteous tears but God had changed her heart. And in that instant, the Little Way of Spiritual Childhood was born. It was a way of love, trust and self-forgetfulness.

Now love and trust are characteristic of a normal child whereas self-forgetfulness is not. Thérèse says her heart was filled with charity, making her forget herself. This should alert us to the fact that Thérèse's desire to become little, even increase in littleness, is in no way a desire to return to swaddling clothes. Rather it is a desire to become the spiritual child commended by Christ in the Gospel.

Jesus does not use the word "spiritual" but he does use another word that gives us a clue to the meaning of this much discussed text. He says, "Unless you turn and become *like* little children." So we are exhorted not to *become* children, with all the immaturity that implies; rather we are invited to rediscover, as adults, the spiritual strengths of the child.

Moral theology distinguishes between natural and acquired virtue. The virtues of a small child – love, trust, dependence – are natural, not something the child has acquired by conscious effort. The virtues of spiritual childhood, on the other hand, are all acquired. It takes practice and perseverance to become a spiritual child.

So we can be reassured at the outset: contrary to various misrepresentations of Thérèse's message, our saint is not selling some kind of beatified babyhood. "I am a baby," admits Thérèse, "but a very old one, a baby who knows a thing or two!"[3]

As far as spiritual childhood goes, Thérèse seems to know just two things: the imitation of the child and the imitation of Christ. Her choice of religious names bears witness to this: Sr Thérèse of the Child Jesus and of the Holy Face. Her twofold aim is to be a child in God's arms and to look for strength and inspiration to Christ the Redeemer. She is a child but a child who walks in the steps of Christ crucified. This is the true meaning of spiritual childhood.

Now it is a curious fact that many Christians regard the way of spiritual childhood as optional whereas Christ makes it quite clear that it is an essential qualification for entry into his kingdom. Unless we become like little children, we *cannot enter the kingdom of heaven.*

So what are little children like? They are simple and straightforward, full of wonder. They are trustful and unconcerned about the future; they live intensely in the present moment. They are totally dependent on their elders. They forgive freely and neither judge nor condemn.

We know, of course, that little children have other characteristics: a short attention span, a tendency to stamp their tiny feet and to yell, a certain lack of foresight and prudence. Clearly when Christ commended a child as a model, he was thinking of its strengths rather than its weaknesses.

As we study the strengths of the child, we shall discover that each of these strengths may be seen, developed to perfection, in the life of Christ. So let us now examine just three of the child's traits: simplicity, wonder and trust.

God is essentially simple. He is pure being: I AM. Christ, the express image of the Father, is also simple. The briefest glance at the gospels will confirm this.

The only recorded words of Christ's early years, "Did you not know that I must be about my father's business?" reveal the single-mindedness of true simplicity. He has only one aim, to fulfil the divine mission. Later, he must compress the message of God's love into three short years of ministry. His words are simple and direct. He calls people to repent for the kingdom of heaven is at hand and he describes the kingdom in homely parables: sower and seed, birds and beasts, women cooking, men tilling the soil, a father and his sons. All is simple without, however, being easy. What could be simpler, or more profound, than the Lord's Prayer? What could be simpler, or more demanding, than the Beatitudes?

Christ is in fact so simple that there is no gap between his teaching and his person. Instead of describing the Way, indicating the Light, preaching the Resurrection,

34

he can simply declare, "I am the Way... the Light... the Resurrection." Christ urges us to imitate his own directness: "Let your Yes be Yes and your No, No." Let your love of your neighbour be expressed in a simple care for their needs, for when you have loved your neighbour you have loved your God.

Finally Christ leaves us this simple command: "Do this in remembrance of me." God in a morsel of bread! We are so familiar with the idea that its breathtaking simplicity fails to amaze us.

Saint John of the Cross used to say that God had spoken but one word, the personified Word who is Christ. In this Word lies all our hope and all our happiness. And it is in response to this simple Word of God that our salvation lies.

It is difficult for us to respond simply to God. We tend to get complicated; we persist in thinking that it all depends on us. There is but one thing that *does* depend on us and that is the decision to put God first, to simplify our endeavours in accordance with Christ's command to seek first the kingdom of God and his righteousness. All the saints did this. They understood that if they truly put God first, everything else would fall into place. Simple!

If we desire to imitate the simplicity of God, we have a sure guide in Thérèse to whom an old nun remarked "Your soul is extremely simple. When you are perfect," she added, "you will be simpler still."[4]

Thérèse had not always been simple. As a child and an adolescent she had tended to fret over her sins, real and imagined. She had suffered from the painful self-consciousness that is the opposite of simplicity. Then, at her conversion, a lot of her complication had fallen away, leaving her with the simple aim of pleasing God.

Thérèse made great strides in simplicity between her conversion and her entry into Carmel but it was not easy for her. Her difficulties, however, have made it easier for us; as we watch her struggling and overcoming, we are encouraged to strive on our own account.

At first we may be surprised at the small scale of Thérèse's conflicts; there are no heroics here, just the daily overcoming of herself in small ways. For Thérèse is a saint of little things and it was her genius to recognise the importance of detail. If we think of it, we shall probably concur that it is the details that so consistently trip us up. For example, the young Thérèse was not content simply to perform little acts of kindness; she wanted to be thanked! Many of us are like that. Of course it is nice to be thanked but it is even nicer if we can give without demanding the wages of appreciation. The simple soul just gives for the sake of giving.

In her early days in Carmel, Thérèse admits that, far from approaching life simply, she would make a fuss about anything and nothing. This is normal in the novitiate; one is learning a new way of life whose demands are constant and often perplexing. However, the aim of the monastic life is essentially simple: God. And God himself is so simple that he can be defined in one word: Love. Thérèse understood this ever more clearly. Her prayer and indeed her whole life became a simple looking at God, both in times of consolation and desolation. She did not read prayers from books but behaved like a small child who could not read; she just said quite simply what she wanted to say and felt that God always understood. When her soul was in darkness, she would have liked to soar to heaven like an eagle but recognised that she was more like a feeble fledgling; she would have to stay beneath the clouds, looking up in simple faith, sure that her Sun was there even if she could not see him.

Thérèse grew simpler and simpler. As her life drew to a close, she tells us she could no longer desire anything ardently except the will of God. Her ambition was both simple and sublime: to love, to be loved and to make Love loved.

With Thérèse the simplification process was a gradual one as it will doubtless be with us. At first, she rather surprisingly continued to search for her true vocation. Was not the monastic life for which she had fought and pleaded so vigorously, not enough for her? Apparently not. She felt in her heart a multitude of vocations: warrior, prophet, priest, apostle, teacher, martyr. She was the child Thérèse again, wanting to march off with the whole basket, declaring, "I choose everything!" Of course she could not choose all those vocations; it was a logical absurdity. But Thérèse never worried about logic; Jesus' love for her was hardly logical either and if he loved her to the point of madness, she would love him likewise. All the same, the pull of these diverse callings was a real torment to her. How would Jesus respond to her madness?

Christ responded by directing Thérèse to 1 Corinthians chapters twelve and thirteen. Chapter twelve explained that not everyone could be apostles, prophets, teachers and so on; the Church was a body composed of different members. That was clear enough but failed to satisfy Thérèse. She read on and found her answer in that magnificent poem to love that is 1 Corinthians chapter thirteen.

Love, Thérèse understood, was the source of all vocations. Love was the heart, supplying the lifeblood to every member of the Church. Without love, the whole Christian enterprise would founder. The apostles would no longer proclaim the Gospel, the martyrs would refuse to shed their blood. At last Thérèse had found her vocation, the love that inspired and contained every other vocation. Thérèse, who never did anything by halves, decided that she would be love. Her ambition was not to become more loving or to live in love, but to *be* love. With audacious simplicity, Thérèse resolved to be exactly what God is: love.

Thérèse recounts that she discovered her true vocation in an excess of delirious joy but she was not delirious enough to imagine that she could "be love" in her own strength. A weak and helpless child, she would be the victim of divine love. Love, she explains, is only fulfilled in self-abasement, the abasement of a God who stoops to transform into fire our human nothingness. To be a victim of love was to allow God to love through her.

The simplicity of children is closely related to another childhood trait: wonder. Again, Christ is our example here.

What a mystery! The divine Word, co-creator of the universe, becomes a child who gazes in wonder at a world of his own fashioning. We can imagine the child Jesus as he discovers the countryside around Nazareth: the brilliant lilies of the field, the sparrows over which God watches, the full ears of corn, oxen and donkeys at their daily labour. He feels the rhythm of the seasons and rejoices in the beauty of spring, the heat of summer, the gladness of the harvest and the chill of winter. Everything speaks to him of his heavenly father.

Christ's wonder is not confined to natural phenomena. As an adult, he wonders at the beauties to be found in human life: the miracle of penitent Magdalene, the faith of the centurion, the gratitude of the Samaritan leper, the trust of Peter, the devotion of John. So it is not surprising that his saints, too, should be men and women of wonderment.

"I have marvelled at the depths of his wisdom, I have experienced his goodness and mercy, I have perceived the excellence of his glorious beauty and I am filled with awe and wonder at his manifold greatness" thus St Bernard in a sermon. And St Augustine, in more corporeal mode, asks, "What do I love when I love God? I love light, melody, fragrance, food and embrace!"

Thérèse, too, was a soul filled with wonder. She inclined more to St Bernard in this than to St Augustine. Food would probably not have figured on her list for she seems to have been indifferent to it. But melody, fragrance and embrace are all things that led her to praise God. She was not musical herself but enjoyed music and urged others to make their lives a melody to their Creator. Thérèse loved fruit and flowers and appreciated scent so much that on her deathbed she remembered guiltily a bottle of cologne; maybe she had enjoyed it too much? Usually she had no such scruples and like her saintly mother Teresa, she would have prayed,

"Let me care for naught beside thee, *except insofar as it will lead me to thee.*"[5]

"Embrace" was certainly an aspect of human life that spoke to Thérèse of God. When she was caressed on earth, she would imagine the caresses she would one day receive in heaven. When she marvelled at the love of her earthly father, she thought spontaneously of her father in heaven.

As Jesus marvelled at created beauty in nature and human life, so did Thérèse. As a child she loved to gaze at the night sky and in a moment of unconscious prophecy she once pointed to the T-shape in Orion and exclaimed, "Look, Papa, my name is written in heaven!" Thunderstorms held no terrors for her; she revelled in them, seeing in celestial fireworks the splendour of God. The sea, too, spoke to her of God's boundless majesty. Sometimes as she sat by the river on a summer day, her thoughts would turn from the beauty of earth to the wonders of heaven.

When Thérèse made her first and last long journey, the pilgrimage to Rome, she wanted to store up all the beauties of the trip for future delectation. She found in the alpine scenery a foretaste of heavenly beauty, yet there is a slight wistfulness as she remarks that soon she will be a prisoner in Carmel, seeing only a corner of earth and sky. God accepted her sacrifice of worldly beauty but he is never outdone in generosity. Thérèse was to find fruit and flowers in Carmel and during her last illness she was cheered by a friendly robin hopping on her windowsill.

Keenly alive to natural beauty, Thérèse wondered even more at the workings of God's grace in human hearts. As a novice, she was quick to perceive true holiness in the serene faith of Mother Geneviève, one of the foundresses of the Lisieux Carmel. One day the old nun urged Thérèse to serve God in peace and joy. Thérèse had been depressed that day, even doubting God's love but she was sure that she hadn't shown her feelings so she asked if her spiritual mentor had had a special revelation of Thérèse's state of mind. Apparently that was not so and Thérèse concluded that Jesus lived in the old nun's heart and had inspired her to offer a timely word of encouragement. Mother Geneviève, thought Thérèse, was a soul made holy by hidden and ordinary virtues. It was the sort of holiness that appealed to Thérèse, as it was free from illusion. It was in fact the kind of sanctity that was later to be found in Thérèse's Little Way.

Thérèse was often deeply moved by the thought of God's love. Once her sister Céline found her working in her cell, her eyes glistening with happy tears. She had just been thinking how wonderful it was to be able to call God "father", explained Thérèse. On another occasion, when a novice whom she had reproved, came and apologised, Thérèse shed tears of joy; if she, Thérèse, felt such love for a contrite Sister, what must God feel for the sinner who returns to him?

The wonder of a small child results quite naturally in trust. It trusts its parents, those wonderful creatures who know everything! Sooner or later comes the horrible realisation that one's parents and elders are fallible. Fortunately, we have a heavenly father who continues to deserve our trust. Once again, Jesus is our example here.

Christ always trusted his heavenly father but it would be a mistake to assume that such trust always came easily to him. If it is true that Christ emptied himself of his divine prerogatives, that he grew in wisdom and stature, it follows that he had to grow in trust. For example, we see him as a twelve-year-old boy amid the doctors of the Temple. "Did you not know that I must be about my father's business?" he asked a bewildered Mary and Joseph. While it seems that Jesus sensed his divine sonship at that time, it is unlikely that he realised exactly where his "father's business" would lead him. So he needed to exercise trust in the guidance of God. It was during the hidden years at Nazareth that he was to develop that trust.

It is by trusting that one learns to trust. For example, Jesus had to trust in God's timing. Thirty years is a long apprenticeship and three years is a short time in which to persuade a blind and hardened world of the love of God. And when his ministry was at last underway, Christ had to trust his father for strength and wisdom at every step. He needed wisdom to choose his apostles and he needed trust in God when those same apostles betrayed, forsook and denied him. He needed trust as he hung on the cross, apparently abandoned by God. Between Jesus' cry "My God, my God, why have you forsaken me?" and his "Into your hands I commend my spirit", there lies a gulf of anguish. It is because Christ triumphantly traversed that gulf that we, too, are able to cling to God in times of darkness and despair.

Throughout her life, Thérèse grew in trust. As a child, she was struck by the words of Job, "Though he slay me yet will I trust him." When Thérèse first encountered these words, she had already suffered her first bereavement, the loss of her mother at the age of four-and-a-half. More bereavements were to follow as her two mother substitutes, Pauline and Marie, left her to enter Carmel. Each time the little girl suffered terribly. Why was it that God took away the people she loved best?

The mature Thérèse was able to affirm that even the smallest events of our lives are ordered by God. Before arriving at such trust, she had to pass, she tells us, through the crucible of suffering. There were the miseries of school, the agonies of shyness, her intractable habit of weeping at the slightest provocation and then weeping for having wept. She also suffered from scruples, which are basically a lack of trust in God. If we trusted God as our loving father, we would hardly imagine that he was forever ready to condemn our slightest misdeeds.

Towards the end of her life, Thérèse was to thank God for allowing her to suffer. Like Christ, she had learned obedience through the things she had suffered, that obedience which is so closely related to trust. For obedience is much more than doing as one is told; it is an attitude that enables us to hear and respect God's ordering of our lives and to trust that it is an ordering of love.

As a nine-year-old Thérèse had felt that life was one long suffering, one long separation. Later she was to see that life could also be one long lesson in trust. Thérèse learned her lesson gradually but she learned it well. Through the loss of her mother and two successive substitute mothers, she learned to trust in her heavenly mother, Mary. She also learned to trust in the motherliness of God who, she affirms, has a heart more tender than that of any earthly mother. When lonely at school, she used to go to the chapel to be with Jesus, trusting in his real presence in the Blessed Sacrament. As for her scruples, she trusted her dead brothers and sisters to pray for her deliverance, and they did. And we have already seen her overcoming her hypersensitivity by the supreme act of trust that preceded her Christmas conversion of 1886.

Even after Thérèse had regained her "strength of soul" at the age of fourteen, she still had many lessons to learn in trust. First of all there was the question of her religious vocation. To enter Carmel at the age of fifteen did not appear a prudent move. Prudence, in the shape of Uncle Guérin, the convent chaplain, the bishop, even her own sister Marie, rose up in opposition. But Thérèse had received a clear call from God; trustfully she went ahead. She dared to plead with the Pope on the subject and was devastated when he, too, returned a prudent answer: she would enter if it was God's will. Thérèse went on trusting. She said she felt like a plaything in the hands of the Christ Child. She was a little ball, which he could throw aside or even pierce to see what was inside. This was no sentimental nursery image but an expression of Thérèse's trust in the God who, having called her, had apparently abandoned her.

When at last Thérèse had stormed the citadel of Carmel, her trust was to be tested once more. Mother Marie de Gonzague, the prioress, hitherto so kind and encouraging, became severe and demanding. "One can see that our cloisters are swept by a fifteen-year-old child!" she once sniffed. Later, Thérèse was thankful not to have been the spoilt baby of the community but at the time it was hard to be the butt of constant criticism. She needed to trust that "all things work together for good for those who love God."[6]

A much greater test of trust awaited Thérèse and her sisters: the mental illness of their beloved father. Louis Martin had already suffered a slight stroke before Thérèse's clothing as a novice. However, he had been well enough to attend the ceremony. Thérèse noted sadly that it was his last feast day here below. Worse was to follow: further strokes, mental confusion, a habit of wandering off, sometimes for days at a time. Finally Monsieur Martin was admitted to a mental home in Caen. In Thérèse's day, mental illness was considered shameful. People whispered, outside and within the convent: it was Thérèse's fault; by entering the convent she had broken her father's heart and unbalanced his mind. Through her tears, Thérèse saw things differently. Was not her father following in the steps of Christ the Suffering Servant, the one who was despised and rejected? She could entrust her beloved parent to God.

Usually a novice would make her religious vows after a year's novitiate but Thérèse's vows were delayed for eight months. Again she had to trust that she would indeed make her vows in God's good time.

At the age of twenty, Thérèse was entrusted with the job of assistant novice mistress. This was in any case a daunting task for so young a nun. It was made into a veritable minefield by the jealous interference of Mother Marie de Gonzague. Thérèse, with her customary realism, acknowledged that the task was beyond her strength. Trustingly she turned to Jesus; she would take counsel with him and then advise her charges accordingly. She kept her eyes firmly on Christ and said she would instruct her novices without even turning round.

When Thérèse made her vows, she asked Jesus to grant her martyrdom of heart or body, or rather both. Her prayer was answered.

For many years Thérèse had suffered dryness in prayer. But that is par for the course, as any nun will tell you. If nuns were perpetually basking in spiritual consolation, they would perhaps deserve the world's taunt that they have chosen an easy and irresponsible path.

But it is one thing to experience dryness in prayer, quite another to be confronted with total blackness, a dense spiritual fog, a wall reaching up to heaven itself. It happened to Thérèse shortly after the first haemorrhage that heralded her death from tuberculosis. Far from being alarmed, Thérèse was jubilant at the thought of going to heaven. She could not believe that there were people without faith. Immediately after this, she was plunged into a spiritual night that was to last until the hour of her death. The thought of heaven, hitherto so sweet, became a subject of torment. She was headed, she felt, for an even deeper darkness: annihilation.

Up to this point in Thérèse's life, her trials had been experienced against the background of her faith. Now that background simply dissolved. She still wrote poems expressing a radiant faith; no one could have guessed at the darkness that invaded her soul, the mocking demonic voices inviting her to despair. And when she spoke to the chaplain of her temptations against the faith, he warned her that her case was extremely dangerous: not a great help! She spoke once to her sister Marie about it: "Do *you* have temptations against the faith?" Marie, shocked, answered that of course she didn't!

Thérèse felt very much alone and then she realised that she was not alone after all. She was in the company of all those who do not believe. She called it "the table of sinners". Maybe God was calling her to sit at that table, eating its bitter bread; maybe the presence of one loving soul would eventually lead all the others to the light, that light in which she still trusted although it was hidden from her eyes Thérèse thought that God and the saints were waiting to see how far she would trust.

The first part of her prayer had been answered: she had been granted martyrdom of heart. Martyrdom of the body was soon to follow.

In Thérèse's day, tuberculosis was almost invariably fatal. There were various treatments, mostly very painful, usually useless. Thérèse endured these without much hope of a cure. Morphine injections were sometimes given but Mother Marie de Gonzague considered these a soft option for a Carmelite, so the most Thérèse was allowed as a palliative was syrup of morphine. "It is atrocious, what she is suffering!" exclaimed the doctor. But Thérèse continued to trust "Papa le Bon Dieu". She even assured her sister Pauline that she was happy. She laughed and joked with her visitors and it was only when she was alone with her own sisters that she would allude to her spiritual and physical torment. Pointing to a shadowy patch of garden, she confided to Pauline that she was in a black hole like that, soul and body. But she was at peace. Thérèse's peace was the peace of Christ in Gethsemane: "Your will, not mine, be done!" It was the peace of Christ who having cried, "My God, why?" bowed his head and entrusted his soul to his father's hands.

A few minutes before she died, Thérèse declared, "I

know that God will not abandon me … I do not regret having given myself to Love."[7] Thérèse's trust, like her martyrdom, was complete.

It is inspiring to observe Thérèse as she sought to imitate Christ and to reproduce in her own life his simplicity, wonder and trust, for Thérèse's standard is high; it is the standard of Christ himself. But to hear Thérèse describing her Little Way of Spiritual Childhood, on the other hand, may come as a disappointment. Perhaps we are suffering from "Naaman's syndrome", that is, the inability to accept a simple solution to our problems. It was Naaman who sought a cure for his leprosy at the house of the prophet Elisha[8]. The prophet was a big disappointment to his petitioner who had expected an audience with the holy man. Instead, Elisha merely sent a message: go and dip yourself seven times in the Jordan. Naaman felt it beneath his dignity to dip in a river, a dirty Israeli river at that. And yet, when his servants persuaded him to follow the prophet's advice, his skin became like the skin of a little child.

Thérèse's solution to the problem of holiness is simple, too. And it seems beneath our dignity. That is, of course, one of its chief merits; it strips us of our false dignity and dips us in the cleansing waters of God's love, from which we emerge with the "skin of a little child". That is, we begin to shed our layers of sophistication, our complicated methods of approaching God.

Thérèse herself had once favoured a complicated approach to God. We have seen her as a small child, constantly fingering her rosary of practices, recording her slightest good deed. Later, she fell into the snare of scrupulosity, which is an exaggerated attention to one's slightest faults. The first is a positive use of small things, the second a negative. Thérèse does not forsake the small things but transfigures them. No longer will she eagerly compute her merits or agonise over her demerits; instead she will use every detail of her daily life as a means of union with God.

The more we study Thérèse, the more we shall wonder if she was indeed little. Did not a pope describe her as "the greatest saint of modern times"? Perhaps Thérèse is just being modest when she uses the word "little"? No, Thérèse is stating a simple truth but perhaps the word "little" is misleading. "Ordinary" would probably be more accurate. Thérèse is saying that everything about her is ordinary: her background, her education, her prayer, her reactions to the minor frustrations of daily life. Thérèse's greatness lies in her grasp of the fact that littleness, ordinariness, can be the material for holiness; it is not necessary to be a high-flier to be a saint. Thérèse flew low and she invites us to do the same. The secret is to become like a little child.

In seeking to imitate the child, Thérèse follows a well-established biblical tradition. The children of the Bible are depicted as innocent and humble, trusting and obedient. We watch Isaac as he accompanies his father to Mount Moriah[9]. He asks him one question and then falls silent, trusting that God will indeed provide the young animal for the sacrifice. Then there is the child Samuel, turning obediently towards the darkness of the temple: "Speak, Lord, for your servant is listening."[10] There is the boy David, hastily summoned from the pastures, humbly silent as the prophet anoints him in the presence of his brothers. Both Solomon and Jeremiah plead inability to fulfil their divine mission on the grounds that they are mere children. Solomon humbly requests an understanding heart and Jeremiah is told, "Whatsoever I command you, you shall speak... I have sent you... to root out and to pull down and to destroy and to throw down, to build and to plant."[11] Thérèse had a similar mission: she was to root out the last vestiges of Jansenism from fearful hearts; she was to destroy the notion that saints' lives must be full of ecstasies and miracles; she was to throw down the mathematical theory of good deeds; she was to build confidence in God's loving kindness and plant the desire for holiness in the hearts of ordinary people. She had the trust of Isaac, the obedience of Samuel, the humility of David, the discernment of Solomon, the missionary spirit of Jeremiah. Unlike them, however, she was to do no great deeds in her lifetime; on earth her glory would not be seen by mortal eyes. Instead, she was to become a great saint by walking in the way of spiritual childhood.

When we learn that Thérèse had felt at the age of fourteen that she was born for the glory of sainthood, we may be astonished, perhaps shocked at her boldness. Yet it is this boldness that is the very foundation of her Little Way. It is the boldness of a small child.

A small child is bold in its demands just because it believes that its parents are omnipotent. It is often bold, too, with regard to its own powers. Infants have been known to stride into the sea, quite unafraid, and many a child has cherished the illusion that it could fly if it just flapped its arms. Thérèse takes the boldness of the small child and transposes it onto the spiritual plane. Her heavenly father is omnipotent so of course he can make her a great saint! She need not fear the waves of suffering; she can fly to God on the wings of faith and trust.

Thérèse knows that her God is a God of boundless love, of infinite spiritual riches, so she makes bold requests. She asks and receives in the spirit of the gospel. She asks for a sign of repentance from the obdurate criminal Pranzini. She asks for spiritual light for herself and her novices. Perhaps her boldest demand is the one she makes of the saints and angels: that she might have *a double portion of their love.* Holiness, for Thérèse, is to be humble and small in God's arms, aware of our weakness but confident to the point of boldness in his fatherly goodness.

So profound was Thérèse's trust in God's goodness that she dared to ask that at her death she might go *without delay* to God's arms. She could not believe that childlike souls would suffer purgatory, much less be damned. Her entourage was not sure about either point. There were indeed an astonishing number of her contemporaries who lived in fear of both purgatory and hell. Jansenism had doubtless led many to an exaggerated notion of God's demands. Obviously if one didn't come up to scratch, one would not gain heaven. Thérèse, while boldly aiming at being perfect as the heavenly father is perfect, freely acknowledged her own weakness and inability to reach holiness unaided. But with a double portion of heavenly love, the sky was the limit! Besides, she did not ask God to count her works; she knew that "all our righteousness is filthy rags"[12]. Instead, she boldly asked God to be himself her sanctity. How could her heavenly father refuse such a request? How could she live in fear of a divine justice that would weigh her life in the balance and find it wanting?

Unafraid and full of confidence, Thérèse grew ever bolder. When her autobiography was circulated after her death, one monastic superior expressed shock at the young nun's audacity. "Had she lived longer", opined the good mother, "she would have modified her views." That seems unlikely. Thérèse's views did not arise from the temerity of uninstructed youth; they were solidly based on Scriptures texts such as these:

"Exceeding great and precious promises are given to us: that by these you may be partakers of the divine nature."[13]

and

"All things are yours... the world, or life or death or things present or things to come. And you are Christ's and Christ is God's."[14]

Thérèse's boldness sprang, not from self-confidence but from a boundless trust in God's mercy and strength. She never lost sight of her weakness and could have repeated with St Paul,

"I am the least ... but by the grace of God I am what I am."[15]

Thérèse admired the loving audacity of Mary Magdalen, the penitent trust of the publican, the firm avowal of Peter, who dared to say after his three denials, "Lord, you *know* that I love you!" She also identified with the Prodigal Son; even had she committed every possible sin, she tells us, she would have thrown herself into Jesus' arms, knowing his love for those who return to him.

Thérèse did not merely read Scripture; she appropriated it. She loved to repeat Mary's words "The Almighty has done great things for me." For Thérèse, the greatest thing that God had done, she said, was to show her, her own nothingness.

Most audacious of all was Thérèse's appropriation of John chapter seventeen. How did she dare to do what no one else has ever done: apply to herself Jesus' last long prayer? Probably she was thinking of the words of the father in the parable of the Prodigal Son, "All that I have is yours."[16] So Thérèse felt free to appropriate this beautiful prayer. She omits the passages that apply to Christ alone, but she makes her own several of Christ's petitions, ending with "And may the world know that you have loved them as you have loved me." Always Thérèse had the same ambition: to love, to be loved and *to make love loved.*

In all this, Thérèse shows the trustful audacity of a small child who is sure of her father's love. She is bold but she is also reverent. Like Julian of Norwich, she is "homely" with God "without leaving courtesy."[17]

Because Thérèse was unafraid of her heavenly father, she was able to grow more and more in the virtue of abandonment. Little children abandon themselves naturally to the care of their parents. Even in the midst of danger, a small child will sleep peacefully in its mother's arms. Thérèse would have appreciated the true story of the small

50

boy who was seen playing happily on the deck of a ship during a violent storm. When asked if he was not afraid, the little fellow replied, "No. My father is the captain."

We soon lose this natural *insouciance* and most of us spend a great deal of time fending off the various assaults of life. We also expend much energy in worrying: how are we to achieve our goals, finish our work, make something worthwhile of our lives? Thérèse learned to abandon all these concerns to God. This made her vulnerable both to God and to her companions. You can do anything you like with a small child. Thérèse allowed God to do just as he liked with her: consolation or desolation, spiritual illumination or dense fog, health or sickness. "It is what he does that I like", declares Thérèse.

Abandoned to God's will, Thérèse was also abandoned to the will of her Sisters. She often allowed others to take advantage of her generosity ("Give the leftovers to Sr Thérèse, she never complains.") The novices interrupted her at all hours of the day with questions, demands, complaints. Most of the Sisters, recounts Céline, consulted Thérèse at one time or another. The older ones came, like Nicodemus, in secret; after all, Thérèse was only in her twenties and they had years of monastic life behind them so it wouldn't do to be seen seeking her counsel! Then there were the poems to celebrate feasts and anniversaries; everyone wanted one. Thérèse scribbled her compositions on the backs of old envelopes; she wrote fifty-four poems in all, most of them at the request of others.

When Thérèse was too ill to join in community life, she would sit in her wheelchair in the garden, writing her autobiography. A novice would creep up to whisper some confidence in her ear. Hardly had she gone when a kindly Sister would bring her a bunch of flowers and another would stop for a chat, "Just to distract you a bit!" Thérèse was distracted all right. She happened to be writing about charity so she tried to practise what she was preaching.

Even on her deathbed, there was little peace for Thérèse. There were endless visitors. Most of these were well-wishers but there was one Sister who would stand at the foot of the bed and laugh mockingly. Thérèse smiled bravely but it must have been unnerving, to say the least.

It must have been unnerving, too, to have her own sisters taking notes of her least utterance as she lay dying. It is wonderful for us to have such a detailed account but it must have been daunting, or perhaps just plain annoying, for the patient! One can sense her utter weariness when, on the eve of her death, Céline begged for a last word. "I have said it all", sighed Thérèse, "Love of one's neighbour is all that matters."[18]

It was the love that Thérèse practised, a love of utter abandonment to the good pleasure of God and her companions, a love that, like Christ, she practised until the end.

Thérèse's love was strong and constant but it remained always the love of a spiritual child. It did not express itself in grand gestures, apostolic labours or bloody martyrdom. Thérèse thought of herself as a child throwing flowers to please God. This pretty image hides a profoundly demanding reality. It means, Thérèse explained to the novices, never losing any opportunity of proving one's love for God, always seeking the most perfect thing, practising all the virtues. It is not a way of idleness or comforting pieties. It is not an easy way but it is, as Thérèse desired, a way that is open to everyone.

Thérèse's way is for ordinary people. Whereas her spiritual father, St John of the Cross, has the drama of an el Greco and her mother Teresa the vivid colours of a Raphael, Thérèse is more like a Seurat. Her sanctity is made up of tiny dots, little things, small but nonetheless costly. She is above all the imitable saint. Everyone who really wants to, can walk the Little Way.

4
Thérèse, Contemplative

> Fold your wings, my soul, those wings you had
>   spread wide
> to soar to the terrestrial peaks where light is
>   most ardent;
> it is for you simply to wait the descent of the
>   divine fire –
> supposing it be willing to take possession of you.
>
> *Pierre Teilhard de Chardin*

To many people, contemplation is a daunting word for a daunting activity. Can it in fact be called an activity? It conjures up visions of mystics, holy people wrapped in the enjoyment of God. Perhaps most people do not realise that contemplative monasteries are full of ordinary souls; the Teresas and Angelas of Foligno are few and far between. For every John of the Cross, there are hundreds of pedestrian monastics; they don't hear heavenly voices or fall into ecstasies; they don't even levitate! But they do strive to shape their earthly lives to the pattern of the heavenly life. This true story from America will help to illustrate the point.

Some years ago, a statue of the Madonna was making a tour of American churches and monasteries. The Pilgrim Madonna was greeted with great devotion in a certain house of Poor Clares. Some of the Sisters approached the guardian of the statue and asked, "Does she ever speak to you?"

"Oh yes, every day", he replied.

"Every day!" breathed the nuns "Oh my! What does she say?"

"Well, it's just two words, always the same: Shape up!"

To "shape up" means to conform one's behaviour to a pattern or ideal. This is the original meaning of the word "contemplation". In Sanskrit, the word "temp" was used for a notch made in a piece of wood as a means of measurement. A temple was originally not a building but a measured area on the ground that corresponded to a certain area of the sky. To contemplate (literally to "measure with" or "shape up") meant to order one's earthly behaviour according to signs in the heavens. Sometimes temples were built, like Stonehenge, so that certain heavenly bodies shone on a particular stone at a particular time. Again, if the planets were in a particular position, the priests would advise the king to wage war or cross the sea or take a wife. Always the aim was to conform or shape up the earthly activity to the heavenly. The priests' task was to interpret the heavenly signs; the people's duty was to shape up.

The early Church adopted the hitherto pagan Roman term "contemplation" simply because it fitted so well the Christian aim of doing God's will "on earth as it is in heaven". The Church fathers thought of Moses as a great contemplative not only because he spoke to God face-to-face (that is, he looked at the heavens) but also because he translated his heavenly vision into earthly action. Moses brought the people the Ten Commandments, which were the supreme way of measuring up to God's requirements. He also brought them the building-plan for the temple *as it was shown to him on the mountain*. In other words, he matched the earthly building to the heavenly vision. The temple was a place where one learned to shape one's earthly conduct to God's heavenly will.

Christ, the model of all contemplatives, takes up the idea of the heavenly vision translated into earthly action. He tells us that he does whatever he sees his father doing. He is constantly shaping his earthly conduct to the will of his heavenly father. St Paul, too, speaks of being "obedient to the vision"; he saw Christ and thereafter strove to conform his conduct to the divine will.

Thérèse belonged to the order of Our Lady of Mount Carmel. Carmelites regard Mary as the model contemplative for she corresponded perfectly with the heavenly pattern of redemption when she answered, "Let it be to me according to your word." It was through her that God's heavenly design was carried out on earth.

It is against this background that we shall consider Thérèse the contemplative.

However, having explored the wider significance of the word "contemplation", we should not deny its narrower, technical meaning. Contemplation is a recognised type of prayer: silent, non-discursive, often exercised in dark faith. Thérèse was to devote the few years of her life from the age of fifteen until her death, to this type of prayer. Before that, like the rest of us, she had to learn to pray. She learned her lessons well, so we can look to her with confidence for guidance.

The evolution of Thérèse's prayer is comfortingly normal. True, there were one or two extraordinary moments, but on the whole there was nothing unusual about her prayer. This is what she wanted, she who felt that her mission was to draw little or ordinary souls to God. So let us now consider the various stages through which Thérèse passed.

The first lesson that Thérèse learned was that of any child lucky enough to be born into a truly devout family: God comes first. However, he is not only a God who makes demands on one's time and energies, he is also a tender and loving father. It follows that prayer is not a mere duty but rather a loving relationship. "Prayer", said St Teresa of Avila, "is nothing but a loving exchange with one whom we know to be our lover." A small child expresses this loving communication primarily in words: morning and evening prayers, grace before meals. If these words are to have any meaning, they must be translated into action: being obedient to one's parents and siblings, for example. The words of prayer gradually influence the child's response to God.

Thérèse, like any well-taught Christian child, learned both to say prayers and to follow them up with appropriate conduct. So prayer was not just something she said, it was a way of life. This is not a lesson one learns by logical deduction; it is something one absorbs from the surrounding atmosphere. Prayer is caught, not taught.

As we have seen, Thérèse made her own transition from spoken prayers to action-for-God by means of the rosary of practices. Each good deed was recorded by slipping down a bead of the rosary. The beads were moved in the opposite direction to mark lapses from grace. Thérèse sometimes became confused and awarded herself a "good" bead when she had been naughty. These things happen when one is four years old and striving for perfection. Anyway, the main message got through – to please God one has to pay attention to one's daily behaviour.

Vocal prayer – the Mass, the Rosary, family devotions – played a large part in Thérèse's early life. However, Thérèse also felt drawn to silent prayer. Sometimes she would hide behind the bed curtains to pray. "What do you do there?" asked one of her teachers. "I just think", answered Thérèse. She also "just thought" on the fishing trips with Papa. Sitting in the sun by the river, she would dream of God and eternal life.

Who can say when dreaming ends and prayer begins? Thérèse's schoolteachers thought they could. "Pay attention, Thérèse Martin!" they would admonish when the little girl's eyes drifted away from her missal in church.

Thérèse was never very happy with vocal prayers. She certainly used them, especially when completing her sister Pauline's programme of preparation for first communion, reaching the dizzying total of two thousand, seven hundred and seventy-three aspirations. But vocal prayer was not really her spiritual milieu, nor was the rosary, despite her deep devotion to the Mother of God. In fact, vocal prayer was for Thérèse a springboard to the prayer of silent love. Thérèse probably knew the story of the Curé d'Ars who noticed a man sitting before the tabernacle in his parish church. The priest asked him what he was doing. "I just look at him and he looks at me", came the reply.

Now to describe vocal prayer as a springboard does not necessarily imply that such prayer should be abandoned altogether. Springboards can be used again and again if we want to dive deeper; St Teresa taught that the recitation of the *Our Father* could bring us to the highest union with God. The important thing is that prayer, however elementary, however sublime, is not an end in itself. Our goal should not be to pray well but to live in God's sight and walk in his ways. Prayer is then fully integrated into our life. The psalmist expresses this truth in a verse that is often translated "I give myself to prayer." The original Hebrew is more succinct: "I prayer".

Prayer is a loving relationship with God in Jesus Christ, the one who always intercedes for us and calls us to join in this work. Thérèse did so with enthusiasm. Early in life she had experienced the power of prayer. In her infancy, her distraught parents had prayed her back from the brink of death more than once. The Blessed Virgin had smiled at her and healed her in answer to her sisters' desperate prayers. Her dead brothers and sisters, she believed, had procured for her deliverance from the disease of scruples. She herself boldly undertook to pray for a change of heart in Pranzini the murderer and the Lord heard her.

Thérèse understood that prayer may change things and people but not God. God's purposes for us are unchanging and his gifts "without repentance". What needs changing is ourselves. God's ways of changing us and those for whom we pray, is by the Cross. God showed Thérèse that it was by the Cross that he would give her souls. She understood the sublime vocation of the Christian, "to make up what is lacking to the suffering of Christ in his Body the Church."[1] Christ won salvation for us on the Cross and this salvation is continually mediated through his Body on earth. If we are to be "co-workers with God", we shall join in his redemptive work. He took the raw ingredients of scorn, mockery and cruelty, met them with love and transformed them into salvation. This divine alchemy is not the prerogative of Christ, it is also the duty and joy of the members of his Body. It was a joy that Thérèse was to experience to the full. To suffer out of love, she taught, was the purest happiness.

Before she entered Carmel, Thérèse had realised the relationship between suffering and sanctity. She had felt an attraction to suffering since her first communion but she admits she was eager to suffer for God without really understanding what this would involve. It could hardly have been otherwise as she was only eleven years old at the time. Thérèse's entry into Carmel marks a watershed in her spiritual life. Before that, she had approached spiritual things with great enthusiasm, meditated with delight, devoured religious books and enjoyed uplifting spiritual conversations with Céline. But all that was to vanish almost as soon as she donned her postulant's dress on the threshold of the monastery. Dryness, she tells us, became her daily bread.

No one can live forever on a spiritual "high". Any vocation, when lived out day by day, tends to bring a certain disenchantment, a certain weariness, often real doubt as to the rightness of one's choice. Thérèse suffered from all these, although perhaps "disenchantment" is too strong a word, for she never lost her enthusiasm for the monastic life. She was probably disappointed by the mediocrity of some of her companions, by the pettiness and jealousies apparent in the community. She also suffered one acute attack of doubt about her vocation, on the eve of her profession of vows. However, when her novice mistress had reassured her and the prioress had laughed at her doubts, she was able to make her vows in great peace.

But the dryness in prayer was there to stay and it is helpful to those of us who are similarly afflicted (is there anyone who is not?) to see how she coped with the situation. Thérèse tackles the problem with characteristic simplicity. First of all, she follows St Teresa's advice and recites the Lord's Prayer or the Hail Mary very slowly. This keeps her in the presence of God and helps to focus her attention. St Teresa also exhorts us to "maintain love." Thérèse pictures love as a fire onto which she throws straw and small sticks to keep it alight. Her straw and sticks are a smile, a friendly word when she would rather keep silent or look bored. If she makes her small contributions to the blaze, she finds that the Lord soon makes up the deficiency.

There were one or two extraordinary episodes in Thérèse's life of prayer. Once when she was making the Stations of the Cross, she felt a flaming dart pierce her heart with almost unbearable sweetness. At another time, she remained in a state of profound recollection for several days. But then she returned to her habitual dryness. She felt as if she was in an underground passage but she trusted that it would lead her eventually to the summit of the mountain of Love. She could see nothing clearly and had to walk by faith.

No one could have guessed at Thérèse's interior state by looking at her. The bishop, seeing her as a postulant in the choir, thought of her as a devout and happy child. The poems and plays she composed for the community are full of joy and fervour. Her insights into Scripture are fresh and compelling. Even when she lay dying, one of the nuns remarked, "They say you have never suffered much." For answer, Thérèse pointed to a bright red medicine by her bedside. Her life, she said, had been like that medicine, apparently delicious but in fact bitter to the taste. Yes, Thérèse had tasted much bitterness but she had never become bitter. She had discovered that suffering when joyfully accepted is a sure means of union with Christ.

Thérèse did not arrive at this union all at once. She travelled towards it step by step, sometimes stumbling but always picking herself up and going forward. She had not forgotten her first communion resolution never to give way to discouragement. In Carmel, she admitted that she was not always faithful *but she was never discouraged.* As she went on, she learned to overcome potential sources of discouragement.

Thérèse often fell asleep over her prayers. This is a weakness from which many people suffer. A novice once confessed this, only to be told by a kindly priest, "That is an affliction, my dear, not a sin!" All the same, it is, or seems to be a serious difficulty when one is striving to give oneself wholly to God. At first it worried Thérèse but then she reflected that parents love their sleeping children; why should not God feel the same?

Thérèse, like most people, suffered from wandering thoughts in her prayer time. She learned to use these positively. If other people came to her mind, she simply prayed for them, thus turning distraction into intercession.

Perhaps the most difficult part of prayer is maintaining generosity of spirit. At the beginning, God often gives consolation and sweetness. St Augustine says this is like giving nuts to a small boy in order to attract him. Later on, sweetness and consolation tend to vanish; God is treating us like adults and demanding more of us. Have we been seeking God or merely his gifts? Are we prepared to give rather than to receive?

Thérèse reminded her novices that Christ came to monasteries to find rest and consolation; his friends in the outside world were always complaining! So he did not expect his nuns to join in the chorus of discontent. It was bad enough for God to have to subject us to our time of trial here on earth, without our constantly telling him how miserable we were! We should smile and hide our troubles from him. Worldly lovers, Thérèse observed, were always trying to catch each other's eyes, always seeking a sign of love. Selfless love, said Thérèse, meant being happy to be ignored by the loved one. But very few people would allow Jesus to sleep in their storm-tossed boat; like the apostles, they wanted to wake him up with their urgent requests. For her part, Thérèse was content to let Jesus sleep in her little boat until the great awakening in heaven.

All the same, it was hard for Thérèse to go on loving with very little outward sign of God's presence. She addresses the problem of a silent God with her usual humour and generosity, saying that she had given herself to him, so he was free to do what he liked with her. In more fanciful vein, she likens herself to a little bird unable to soar above the storm like her brother eagles. She had to sit, cold and drenched, with her eyes fixed on heaven. She knew that her Sun was shining; she couldn't see him that was all. And in the midst of her darkness, she could say jokingly to her sisters that Jesus did not stand on ceremony with her; he certainly didn't go to the trouble of entertaining her!

When Thérèse was very ill, one of her sisters advised her not to tire herself by trying to pray. Thérèse reassured her; she was not praying, just looking lovingly at Christ. Often she repeated St Peter's words, "Lord, you know everything; you know that I love you!"

It was difficult for Thérèse to feel in her heart the desire of an eagle to soar heavenwards and to realise that she was just a feeble fledgling, unable to lift off the ground. However, she reminded herself that faith was possible only during our earthly pilgrimage and faith was exercised in darkness and weakness. She did not want to see visions of God and his saints, she said; she was content to wait until heaven. Besides, she felt that she had discovered a little way to heaven; there should be nothing in it that ordinary folk could not imitate.

Until the last months of her life, Thérèse's prayer had been for the most part quite ordinary. She had known consolation and joy, had endured dryness and what she calls "the monotony of sacrifice." Now she was to experience terrifying blackness. "Heaven" was the first word she had been able to read unaided. Now that same word became a source of torment. All her life she had looked forward to heaven: seeing God with Mary and all the saints, being reunited with her loved ones. But now she *no longer believed in heaven!* Mocking inner voices taunted her, saying that the heaven she had dreamt of was not a beautiful land where she would meet her Beloved. Dream on! said the voices. Welcome death, but you will not find what you are looking for; beyond the grave is the darker night of *nothingness!*

Thérèse continued to write poems about heaven and the eternal possession of God but she confessed sadly that she was singing simply of what she *wanted to believe.*

Astonishingly, Thérèse could find even in this desolation, a proof of God's gentleness and mercy. Had this trial come earlier in her life, she felt she would have been plunged into despair. As it was, God had waited until she was not only strong enough to bear it but also able to use it constructively as intercessory prayer.

Thérèse, always given to parables and pictures, now imagined herself seated "at the table of sinners". By "sinners" she meant all those who, for whatever reason, did not believe in God. Obviously such people entertained no hopes of heaven. Thérèse would join them. She would eat with them the bitter bread of unbelief. She would sit there as one who had once seen God's light but was now plunged into the darkness of the unbeliever. She would repeat, for herself and her companions, the prayer of the publican, "Lord, be merciful to me, a sinner!"

Sometimes people imagine that monks and nuns stand aloof from the world: a superior "us" praying for an inferior "them". This is far from the reality. Monks and nuns live a secluded life but only so that they may concentrate all their energies on the work of prayer. If they are true to their vocation they will be like Thérèse, "Love at the heart of the Church", a love that holds the world's joys and sorrows close to the heart of God. They do this by making their souls a thoroughfare along which may pass the whole of humanity, stumbling, falling, laughing, weeping, running to the arms of God. It is hard work to keep the thoroughfare open. There must be no cowardly self-preoccupation. It is so easy, warns Thérèse, to forget the sublime aim of one's vocation and to turn in on oneself. But a merciful God usually orders it so that monks and nuns, far from feeling superior or self-sufficient, do really identify with their suffering brothers and sisters in the outside world. They feel the disappointments and heartaches that are inseparable from the human condition and that penetrate the most solid enclosure walls. They do not pray *for* sinners so much as *with* sinners, for they recognise their own need of God's mercy. By doing this, they are drawn into the very heart of God's redeeming love, the love that emptied itself and became obedient to death, even the death of the Cross.

On Calvary Christ not only interceded for sinners: "Father, forgive them." He also bore in his own body the shame of sin: "he *became sin*", and knew the awful desolation of God's silence: "My God, my God, why have you forsaken me?"

On Calvary, love wrestled with hate, light with darkness, faith with doubt. Out of the conflict Christ rose a conqueror and in his risen body his wounds shone as tokens of victory. He had told his disciples that where he went, they would go too. They would share his works of healing; they would also share his pain. In his power they too would overcome; they too would bear his glorious scars.

This identification with Christ the Redeemer lies at the very heart of contemplative prayer. When the old monastics spoke of *contemplandum et imitandum,* this is what they meant: to look at Christ and to reproduce in one's own life his love and compassion for a suffering world. This is the ultimate "shaping up" of true contemplation and it is not the prerogative of cloistered religious but the duty of all Christians. We are all called, as St Augustine reminds us, to be other Christs. We are all called to mediate God to a world that thirsts for love. All Christians are called to contemplation in the sense of "shaping up" their lives on earth to the pattern of the heavenly. All are called to pray "Your will be done on earth as it is in heaven." All are called to the work of intercession.

Thérèse was, and is, a great intercessor. By her vocation to be "love in the heart of the Church", she sought to influence from within the active members of Christ's Body. She would inspire steadfastness in the missionary, faithfulness in the priest, courage in the martyr. This would be done, not by voicing pious phrases but by practising steadfastness, faithfulness and courage in her own life. "We cannot buy souls with false coin", she used to say. Our contribution to the healthy functioning of the Church's heart may not be visible, but it must be real. It must be a sharing in the travail of the whole of creation as it makes its way back to God.

The largest part of the prayer offered by monks and nuns consists of the Psalms. Thérèse prayed these daily. These songs of Israel give voice to the whole gamut of human emotions. They range from sublime mystical poetry to cries for vengeance and screams of hatred; they include love of God and his law, praise and thanksgiving for his creation. Their mood can be bitter or exultant, full of hope or bowed down with despair. Anyone who prays the Psalms can lift up to God the whole of humanity in its grace and gladness, its weariness and shame. A poet herself, Thérèse must have loved the poetry of the Psalms. But as Romano Guardini reminds us, "Our obligation is not delightful poetry but granite faith." Thérèse had that granite faith which drew particular strength from the Holy Face of Christ.

Towards the end of her life, Thérèse declared that the Holy Face was the foundation of her entire life of prayer. This may come as a surprise to those who associate her only with the Child Jesus. Her full religious name was Thérèse of the Child Jesus and of the Holy Face.

In April 1885, when Thérèse was twelve years old, her own family and that of her Guérin cousins became members of the Confraternity of the Holy Face, founded at Tours in the 1850's. The devotion of the confraternity centred on Veronica's veil which is venerated in St Peter's Basilica in Rome. Tradition gave the name Veronica or "true image" to the compassionate woman who is said to have wiped Christ's face with her veil on the way to Calvary. In gratitude, Christ left his face imprinted on the veil. The aim of the confraternity was to "wipe Christ's face" by making reparation for blasphemy.

Thérèse made this devotion her own. At the start of her monastic life, she tells us that the little flower transplanted onto mount Carmel was to bloom in the shadow of the Cross; the tears and blood of Jesus would be her dew, her sun his adorable face veiled in tears. Like Jesus, she wanted her face to be hidden. She sought to be another Veronica, a true image of Christ.

Thérèse was to see in her beloved father's mental illness, a true reflection of the suffering Face of Christ. As Christ had suffered the depths of humiliation, so did his faithful servant Louis. As mental illness was considered a disgrace at that time, not only did the family suffer shame but also Louis himself, in his more lucid moments, felt deeply humiliated.

Thérèse looked back into her childhood and remembered a mysterious vision she had seen at the age of seven.

Monsieur Martin was away on a trip when Thérèse suddenly saw a man dressed exactly like her father, in the back garden. He was old and bent and had an apron over his face. Her older sisters tried to persuade her that she had imagined the whole thing but the incident was branded on her memory and eight years later, in Carmel, she understood: she had indeed had a premonition of her father's suffering. In the mental home, Louis often covered his face with a cloth and his body was to grow bent and frail.

During her father's illness, Thérèse would go and kneel before the picture of the Holy Face in the Carmelite choir. There she would meditate on Isaiah's song of the Suffering Servant who had no beauty, who was despised and rejected, who trod the winepress alone. Was this not the image of her beloved father?

At first sight this interpretation may seem too audacious. How can we compare the sufferings of our loved ones with those of Christ? But Thérèse is right, because, in his passion, Christ has assumed all human suffering; he has given us a part in his redemptive pain.

Thérèse, too, desired to be without beauty, treading the winepress alone, unknown to all creatures. It was in contemplating the Holy Face, Céline tells us, that Thérèse learned humility and love of suffering, generosity in sacrifice, zeal for souls and detachment. She lived, rather than merely assumed, the title "of the Holy Face". Guy Gaucher comments, "When we mutilate her name, we mutilate her message, to say nothing of her entire life."[2]

It is also important to realise that Thérèse's two names are interdependent. As we cannot separate the Child Jesus from the Redeemer, so we should not separate Thérèse's childlike trust and simplicity from her courageous desire to share in the sufferings of Christ. There is a constant dialogue between the two. Knowing that she is redeemed, Thérèse is able to run towards God with the simplicity of a little child. Pondering on the mystery of the Holy Face, she finds strength to suffer in union with her Saviour. We can follow her here if we will; all the Little Way is adapted to the capacities of little souls, ordinary people.

Not everyone is called to follow Thérèse into deep spiritual darkness but if we are so called, she is a sure guide. She shows us how to lift our hearts daily to God, allowing him to take all our suffering into the great stream of his redeeming grace. Thus we shall become true contemplatives, souls who seek to "shape up" to the pattern of Christ.

5
Thérèse and Love

At eventide they will examine you on love.

St John of the Cross

A surplus of love is necessary to fill up what is lacking of love in this world.

Martin Buber

It was July 1897. Thérèse lay dying in the infirmary while her sister Céline read a passage on the happiness of heaven. Suddenly Thérèse interrupted with: "That's not what attracts me!"

"What is it then?" asked Céline.

"Oh, it's love! To love, to be loved and to make Love loved."[1]

Love! That was the whole meaning of Thérèse's life. It was, in fact, the only thing that interested her. And she longed to pass on to others the lessons she had learnt. If only everyone could understand the immensity of God's tenderness!

No one is born loving. A baby is a creature who demands rather than gives love; it constantly seeks love in the form of attention, comfort, nourishment. Thérèse was no different from any other baby. She yelled, she stamped her little feet, she sobbed when thwarted or disappointed. As love is generally caught, not taught, Thérèse was fortunate in being born into a very loving family. Her father Louis, who adored her, was inclined to spoil his "little queen" but mother Zélie combined affection with a certain amount of discipline. "I am obliged to correct Baby", she writes to Pauline. Her elder sisters also combined firmness with affection and Céline, nearest in age to Thérèse, made sure that Baby didn't get above herself. Once, when Thérèse was accepting universal admiration with casual indifference, Céline snapped, "Anyone would think all this was mademoiselle's due!" Usually Céline and Thérèse were very good friends and later Thérèse was to describe Céline as "the sweet echo of my soul".

Thérèse's home was ideal in many ways. There was discipline tempered with tenderness, adoration balanced by admonition. There was a deep love of God, a great desire to please him, a keen longing for heaven. In fact, there was so much talk of heaven that Thérèse, with the logic of a child, wanted all her loved ones to go there, fast. She would fondly embrace her parents and wish them dead. When admonished, she asked how could they go to heaven if they didn't die first? Really, adults were so unreasonable!

In all, Thérèse had four "mothers". Her birth mother, Zélie, proved unable to nurse her and as nineteenth-century medicine frowned on the use of non-human milk for infants, a wet nurse had to be found. Rose Taillé, who lived in a hamlet outside Alençon, was chosen, and proved excellent. Thérèse's family visited her fortnightly but she naturally regarded Rose as her mother in those early months. Later, when she rejoined the family circle at Alençon, she seems to have made the transition without much difficulty.

As Thérèse recorded in her autobiography, her early childhood had been extremely happy; everything smiled at her and she smiled back. The idyll was to be of short duration for Thérèse was only four-and-a-half years of age when Zélie died. As we have seen, Thérèse was profoundly shocked by this bereavement. Earlier, she had moved from the comforting bosom of Rose to the welcoming arms of Zélie. Now she had to make do with Pauline, who was only sixteen at the time of Zélie's death. Pauline was very much like Zélie in character but all the same she could never really be more than a substitute. Thérèse's fourth mother was to be Marie who took over the maternal role when Pauline entered Carmel five years later. Thérèse had to adjust to four different mothers in the space of nine years, so it is hardly surprising that she should have had problems with personal relationships. The mature Thérèse was able to love generously and happily but it was a love she had learnt in a hard school.

When Zélie died, Thérèse changed overnight. Gone was the happy little friend of all the world and in her place appeared a timorous, weepy child who was only really at ease in the gentle atmosphere of her own home. To such a child, school was inevitably a rude shock. At home, everyone cared; at school, there was a certain indifference to the little queen of the Buissonnets; even those who seemed to care at first, proved distressingly fickle. At home, scholastic successes were greeted with enthusiasm and praise; in the classroom, the precocious Thérèse was the object of jealousy and bullying.

Things were not much better in the playground. Thérèse never enjoyed boisterous games so she would spend school breaks telling exciting home-made stories to an eager audience. Or she would find dead birds and accord them solemn burial while her companions made up a luxuriously tearful cortège. However, the nuns disapproved of both pastimes: no more stories, no more funeral processions! Poor Thérèse couldn't seem to please. The only real respite was the joyful return each evening to the bosom of the family.

Thérèse's schooldays come under the heading of 'Painful Years' in her autobiography. But there were moments of great joy, too. There was Céline's first communion, when Thérèse was almost as delighted as Céline herself. There was Thérèse's own first communion when she gave herself rapturously to Christ: "I love you and I give myself to you forever!"[2]

For Thérèse it was certainly easier to give herself

wholeheartedly to God than to human beings; you knew where you were with the Lord! Human beings were much more problematical. There was the little school friend who seemed so affectionate but later became cold and indifferent. And there were all those mothers who kept disappearing!

When Thérèse overheard the news of Pauline's projected departure for Carmel, she says it was as if a sword had pierced her heart. This may sound exaggerated but it was probably an accurate enough description of her feelings; it was a painful shock to an emotionally fragile child. Thérèse began to look on life as a continual suffering and separation.

More suffering was to come. Apparently as a result of the emotional jolt of Pauline's departure, Thérèse fell dangerously ill with a strange nervous complaint, possibly chorea. Panic-stricken and sometimes delirious, the young patient began to lose trust in her loving family, hitherto such a refuge in times of distress. Sometimes she thought they were trying to poison her; at other times she failed to recognise them.

At last the Blessed Virgin intervened, smiling at Thérèse and healing her. Gradually Thérèse regained her strength but she was to remain emotionally fragile for three more years. Delivered from the physical suffering of her illness, she fell into the spiritual suffering of scruples, with which she battled for eighteen months. In vain did Marie listen to the daily list of Thérèse's imagined faults, reassuring her little sister and firmly selecting one or two real sins as matter for sacramental confession. Thérèse continued to torment herself over her simplest thoughts and deeds. She wept, she agonised, she found only momentary relief in confiding in Marie; then her martyrdom would begin again. For scruples are indeed a martyrdom, the worst sort, where one suffers agony of mind and witnesses, not to faith in God but to a sad lack of trust. No wonder St Teresa remarked briskly, "God is not concerned with a heap of trifles!"

In the end, Thérèse did what she had done with her

illness: finding no help on earth, she turned to heaven. She asked her four dead brothers and sisters for help. Able to delve into the divine treasury, they would be able to find her some peace. They did. Thérèse was freed from her scruples and rejoiced that she was loved in heaven as well as on earth.

Up to this point, Thérèse had been largely on the receiving end of love. This was natural and normal; none of us can learn to love unless we are first loved. However, if love is to mature beyond the childish level, one must reverse the flow. "I am loved" must give way to "I love". With most people this is a gradual, almost imperceptible process. With Thérèse it happened overnight, with her "complete conversion."

On that Christmas morning of 1886, Thérèse reached a watershed in her apprenticeship of love. Up to that time, she had toiled upwards, burdened by her hypersensitivity, tearful, self-absorbed. Then love entered her heart and she forgot herself in order to please others. All the love she had received – God's love, the love of a patient and supportive family – began to flow in the opposite direction. Now she would make giant strides towards the God who is love.

It was at this time that Thérèse began to understand and respond to the demands of God's love. "I thirst!" cried Christ on the Cross. Thérèse interpreted the divine thirst as a desire for souls, a desire that found an enthusiastic echo in her own heart.

Thenceforth she would never keep graces for herself. Instead she would pour them out for the benefit of souls. She would pray fervently and obtain the conversion of the murderer Pranzini. She would teach the truths of the faith to the three motherless children whom the Martins took into their home for a while. She would be a contemplative nun and devote her life to bringing souls to the knowledge of the love of God.

When Thérèse entered Carmel as a fifteen-year-old she

wanted to give her heart exclusively to Jesus. No one else would have an atom of her love! The young novice worked hard to achieve this ideal. Like all novices, she would dearly have loved to turn to human support as she met the trials and problems of her new way of life. She tells us how she used to cling to the banisters on her way upstairs past the prioress' office, determined not to make some excuse to talk to her superior and thus find a few crumbs of human consolation. And poor Marie, her elder sister, assigned to initiate Thérèse into the use of the breviary, was soon despatched with a polite assurance that Thérèse could manage on her own, thank you! Marie was very hurt and later Thérèse was to regret her behaviour. At the time, Thérèse, in her struggle for detachment, had forgotten to practise charity. Gradually she reached a balance in these things.

It was probably necessary for Thérèse to practise detachment at first. In this way, she purified her love. She also learned that, in giving itself to God, the heart does not lose its natural tenderness; on the contrary, its love grows by becoming purer and more divine.

Gradually, Thérèse learned that the only necessary detachment is from oneself. So much of what passes for love is in fact a refined form of self-seeking. One of Thérèse's novices complained that the prioress seemed to enjoy another sister's company more than hers. "And I suffer because I love her so much!" Thérèse pointed out that true love desires the good of the beloved rather than one's own; if the novice really loved the prioress, she would be pleased to see her enjoying another's company.

All this is obvious enough. The only problem is that most of us find it difficult to put into practice. Maybe we could use a refresher course along with Thérèse's novices.

Once Thérèse had become truly detached from self-seeking, she was able to love freely and universally. Towards the end of her life she says she began to understand the meaning of Christ's command to "love as I have loved you". How imperfect was her own love for her sisters when she compared it with Christ's love for her! She now saw that Christ-like love means bearing with others' faults, not being astonished at their weakness, admiring their smallest acts of virtue. And she saw that love should not remain locked in one's heart. Instead, like the lamp of the Gospel, it should be placed on a lamp stand in order to shine on all members of the household.

· This is the difficult part of loving: to love *all* with whom we come in contact. Many people hold the curious belief that the verb to love is a superlative of the verb to like. This is simply not so. We like with our natural inclinations; we love with our will. Liking is morally neutral. To like a person is not more meritorious than, say, to like tomatoes. But to love is a divine commandment: "Love one another as I have loved you."

As Thérèse points out, God never commands the impossible but, left to our own resources, we could never love as Christ loves us. The only solution, she concludes, is to allow Jesus to love within us. This is the very heart of Christianity; we, as the Body of Christ, are to carry on his divine mission of love in our generation. As St Teresa reminds us,

"Christ has no hands on earth but your hands, no feet on earth but your feet."

These words found an enthusiastic echo in Thérèse when she declared that in the midst of the Church she would be love. Now this is not merely a lofty aspiration but also a practical programme. Thérèse realised that love is endlessly inventive; God loves each of us in a unique way, adjusting himself, as it were, to our individuality. One has only to look at the lives of the saints to see how various are the ways of God's loving. God is a "still, small voice" to some, to others a consuming fire, to others a friend or lover. And he loves each soul as if it were the only one on earth. As Thérèse advanced in the ways of love, she began to partake of this divine exclusiveness. She said that she had a heart entirely and wholly for God and yet she also loved each of her sisters entirely and wholly.

This way of loving was not always easy for Thérèse. There was one Sister whom she found disagreeable in every way: her manners, her words, her character. However, thought Thérèse, the Sister in question was a holy nun and doubtless pleasing to God. True charity meant treating that Sister as she would have treated the person she loved most. Thérèse was almost too successful in carrying out this programme. Not only did Sr Saint Augustine become convinced that she was one of Thérèse's favourite people, but Marie Martin took Thérèse aside and warned her against that old monastic snare, "particular friendship".

Another difficult person was fussy Sr Saint Pierre whom Thérèse used to escort to the refectory each evening. It was hard to please this Sister who was in considerable pain and always afraid that Thérèse was going to let her fall. Thérèse smiled and made encouraging noises, arranged her table napkin, cut up her bread and finally won her confidence and gratitude. Thérèse also offered to work in the sewing room with another very difficult Sister; no one else wanted to volunteer for the position. Thérèse set out to comfort and encourage one whom she realised was mentally ill and not responsible for her neurotic behaviour. Why, Thérèse mused, were people so kind and attentive when one was physically ill and so unhelpful when one's ailments were spiritual? Thérèse determined to be a Good Samaritan to the sad and excluded members of the community; after all, they were the ones who most needed love whereas the nuns who were loved most were the gentle and virtuous who needed it least.

If Thérèse had to make a real effort of will to love some of her companions, with others it was easier. There were her blood sisters whom she loved dearly. She could never understand saints who did not love their families. The temptation in the case of the Martin sisters was to show preferential or exclusive love. Thérèse was always very strict with herself on this point; she was determined not to let Carmel become an annexe of les Buissonnets!

There was one Sister with whom Thérèse seems to have been completely at ease – Sr Marie of the Trinity. Thérèse was her novice mistress and showed a maternal love for her, even declaring that it was impossible for her to love Sr Marie more than she did already; her love was so great, it simply couldn't increase! This rather surprising statement shows how far Thérèse had come from her resolution never to give a human being an atom of her love. It also shows a perfect harmony with the teaching of St John of the Cross who regarded detachment from human love as a mere stage of the spiritual journey. Once the initial purification of the affections has been achieved, the great doctor of Carmel teaches that human and divine love can enhance each other. This was evidently Thérèse's experience. At first she had been anxious to love God exclusively; now she realised that the divine commands to love God and neighbour are but one command with two facets. So, in loving human beings, Thérèse never lost sight of God. She even declared that she had never gone three minutes without thinking of God. When the receiver of this confidence showed astonishment, Thérèse remarked simply that one naturally thinks of someone one loves.

Thérèse's whole life could be summed up in one word: love. This is true of all the saints and their love shows an infinite variety, reflecting the infinite riches of the heart of God. There are many saints who, unlike Thérèse, proved their love by mighty works. There was Thérèse's heroine, St Joan of Arc, and the two great Carmelite reformers, St Teresa and St John of the Cross who combined deep contemplation with considerable outward activity. Thérèse was a strictly enclosed contemplative who never left her convent and did not, from the worldly point of view, achieve very much. She was aware that good Catholics, even priests, undervalued the life of contemplative prayer. Like Judas, they complained at the waste of lives poured out, like Mary's precious ointment, at the feet of Jesus. But, says Thérèse, the world is refreshed in spite of itself by the fragrance of the ointment.

Not all of us are contemplatives living a life of cloistered oblation but we can all, in our various vocations, pour out our devotion to Christ. Thérèse was ever insistent that everything she did could be done by little souls or ordinary people. The setting of our life is much less important than the direction of our endeavours. If we are striving to bring our best love to all the details of our lives, we shall be walking along her Little Way. It is a way of hope and humble trust, a way that will lead us step by step to the heart of our loving God.

6

Thérèse, Creative Genius

Christ lived serenely as a greater artist than all other artists, despising marble and clay as well as colour, working in living flesh.

Vincent van Gogh

To believe your own thoughts, to believe that what is true for you in your private heart is true for all – that is genius.

Ralph Waldo Emerson

Genius, according to the Shorter Oxford English Dictionary, is "an extraordinary capacity for imaginative creation, original thought, invention and discovery." By this definition, Thérèse was a genius. She was a mistress of original imagery, she invented a new way to God, she discovered – or rather rediscovered – the very heart of the Gospel message: God is a loving father and we are his beloved children. Yet on the level of general culture, not to mention aesthetic sensibility, Thérèse hardly rises above the mediocre. As her uncle Guérin remarked, Thérèse's schooling was curtailed, her education incomplete. Sometimes she shows a distressing lack of taste; her paintings are sentimental, her poetry often banal, sometimes confusingly overloaded with images and references. What of her *Story of a Soul*? This book has influenced thousands of lives yet its composition is uneven, its style often "school essay"; it lacks polish, with its capitalisation and underlinings. From a literary point of view, it is not an accomplished work of art.

But there is more, much more to Thérèse. Her genius lay in her astonishing ability to create beauty, light and meaning from practically nothing. In this she resembled one of her most original images, the kaleidoscope.

78

When Thérèse was a child, she was curious to discover how her kaleidoscope worked. Dismantling it, she was amazed to find that the procession of beautiful patterns was produced by odd scraps of material reflected in three mirrors. She marvelled at the discrepancy between the means and the end. As an adult, Thérèse saw in the kaleidoscope an image of the Trinity whose threefold nature marvellously transforms our poor human offerings into things of colour and beauty.

Thérèse was herself "kaleidoscopic". She had poor raw material to work with: a narrow background, a scanty education, a lack of theological formation. Even the Carmel that she had so longed to enter, was somewhat disappointing. Although Thérèse charitably avoided saying so, she found a distressing lack of perfection among her religious sisters and the prioress, Mother Marie de Gonzague, turned out to be a capricious and jealous personality. None of this daunted Thérèse. She simply set to work with the materials at hand and, with the help of God, produced that masterpiece of grace that we call sanctity.

This is very encouraging for the rest of us. Thérèse is a living demonstration that sanctity is attainable even with inferior materials and a very narrow range of opportunities. So let us now take a closer look at Thérèse's methods, for as she often repeated, everything she did should be possible for ordinary people like us.

We have described Thérèse as a mistress of original imagery and few would disagree that the kaleidoscope as a picture of the Trinity is unique in the annals of spirituality. Her other images, though less striking, are always apt and evocative.

There is the image of the infant trying unsuccessfully to climb the stairs. This is no sentimental gushing over the poor helpless babe but a realistic picture of the spiritual lives of most of us. We can't do it on our own! As Thérèse's mother stood at the top of the stairs and finally came and carried the baby up, so God tenderly watches our feeble efforts and lifts us up in the end. Thérèse stresses that our efforts, however feeble, are necessary to the enterprise. While sanctity is not a do-it-yourself affair, it is not an armchair occupation either. Thérèse would tell her novices that the infant lifting its foot was a picture of the soul *practising all the virtues*. Only when we do this can we count on God's gracious aid.

Another childhood image – this time taken from Thérèse's own experience – is directed towards those souls who tend to complicate life. Thérèse recounts how she and her friends had tried to go into a garden only to find a large horse blocking the entrance. No one could budge the huge creature. Thérèse found that she was small enough to duck under the belly of the monster: simple! Thérèse was always wary of complicated methods of spirituality. For her, the best road to God was also the simplest.

Thérèse does not merely create images; she uses them to teach a lesson, first to herself and then to others. Above all she opens our eyes to the spiritual lessons to be found in everyday objects and events.

We have already seen how Thérèse discovered, in the Book of Proverbs, the "lift" that would raise her up to God. When she read the words: "Whosoever is little, let him come to me", she saw that it was the arms of Jesus that would serve her as a lift to heaven. No more toiling up the steep stairway of perfection!

When Thérèse read that verse from Proverbs, she was no doubt using the Vulgate translation that has "very small". In fact, the Hebrew word is "simple". However, the general idea of powerlessness is the same and accords exactly with the teaching of St John of the Cross:

> "They alone attain divine wisdom who, like children and ignorant ones, lay aside their own wisdom and serve God in love."

The image of the lift is central to Thérèse's doctrine of the Little Way. We must consent to be small and powerless; and this, Thérèse warns, is what so many souls *will not do!* We naturally like to feel that our spiritual muscles are gaining tone as a result of our spiritual exercises. Thérèse gives us another image to confound this pious hope: the divine eagle and the little bird.

Thérèse would have liked to be an eagle, soaring to heaven like the great saints. Honesty compelled her to admit that she was more like a fledgling, unable to fly high, unable even to see the divine eagle, her Saviour, through the clouds. She would stray from the path, examine wayside flowers, soak her feathers in a puddle. In other words, she was sadly earthbound. Thérèse rejoices in this state of affairs. If she were as large and powerful as an eagle, how would she dare, for example, to fall asleep over her prayers? As it is, she is confident that the divine eagle will lend her his own powerful wings so that at last she may reach heaven. And this, says Thérèse, is the case of all little souls. How she longs to tell them that only one thing is necessary: trust in God's infinite mercy.

This image, like most of Thérèse's images, may not appeal to everyone. However, we should remember that her images are designed less to appeal than to challenge our perception of our own strength. Thérèse discovered early in life that only God's strength could compensate for her weakness. She is eager to pass on the lesson to other little souls.

We have seen the child Thérèse choosing the entire content of the workbasket with the words, "I choose everything!" This was a simple and direct method, she later decided, of arriving at sanctity. One chose everything that God wanted. This meant using everything that God sent, the joys and the sorrows. It meant to profit from one's dispositions, good and bad. In other words, it involved using the raw materials of every day to build a dwelling for

God. And to be indwelt by God is one definition of holiness.

To choose everything that God sends, is to make of life a continual encounter with God. Thus when Thérèse was asked to assist a fretful invalid, she did it as to Christ himself. When she was irritated by the clicking noise made by a neighbour in choir, she pretended that she was listening to a delightful concert that she offered up to God. When she felt a strong antipathy for another Sister, she turned at once to God, reflecting that he, like any artist, enjoyed praise of his work; so she would try to see the disagreeable Sister from God's point of view, appreciating her virtues and showing her as much love as possible. To act in these ways is to use one's imagination creatively instead of becoming angered or depressed by annoying people or circumstances.

On one occasion, Thérèse was justly incensed by the behaviour of the prioress, Mother Marie de Gonzague, who used to invite her relatives to stay at the guesthouse and then require the Sisters to wait on them hand and foot. Thérèse found a happy way to cope with her feelings: she pretended to herself that the guests were the Holy Family. At once her annoyance vanished and she was able to serve them with a will.

All this may sound slightly puerile but Thérèse was concerned less with the means that with the end. If the result of her creative fantasies was more patience and love, that was good enough for her.

Thérèse was very much the daughter of Zélie and Louis, both of whom were creative on the material and psychological levels. Zélie who once described her childhood as "sad as a shroud", refused to wallow in self-pity; instead, she determined that her young brother Isodore should receive the love and warmth that she herself had lacked. Later, Zélie's generous nature sought the life of an apostolic nun, only to be met with the superior's blunt assertion, "It is not the will of God." Very well, Zélie would marry and raise many children for heaven. Before her marriage, she employed her creative talent in mastering the intricate art of lace making. Surely Thérèse inherited from Zélie her ability to create beauty from tiny, almost invisible strands.

As for Louis, he bequeathed to Thérèse the patient attention to detail that is central to the watchmaker's craft. Louis was also a creative opportunist. On one memorable occasion, he met a sick man at Lisieux station. As the sufferer had insufficient funds to return home, Louis promptly removed his own hat, placed a generous donation in it and passed it round to his fellow passengers who, much astonished, also made their contribution and so sent the man safely on his way. Thérèse was to inherit Louis' robust independence of convention. Like her father, if she considered a course was right, she simply went ahead.

That Thérèse went ahead with such speed on the way of sanctity, was surely due to her creative use of all the raw material that came her way. Perhaps the rawest of all was her own character.

Thérèse tells us that with as nature like hers she could have sunk lower than Mary Magdalene. For a "Victorian Miss", Thérèse is sometimes astonishingly blunt! Here she is referring to her passionate nature that was evident from early childhood. She was a soul of strong, even violent feelings. Had these feelings not been channelled to good ends, they might well have led her astray. As it was, her passion became centred very early on God; she longed to love him as he had never been loved before! But first she had to harness the various elements of her nature so that they could work harmoniously.

We have seen Thérèse battling with and finally overcoming her tendency to tearfulness. She describes this battle in some detail in her book. In that particular case, she confronted her undesirable character trait head-on. She forced back her tears and made herself behave cheerfully by an act of the will. But there is another way of mending character faults: the creative use of one's own flaws. It is the method employed by a toper who was found, rather the worse for wear, in a bar.

"Drowning your sorrows?" asked a friend.

"No", came the weary reply, "just teaching them to swim."

When it comes to our own intractable character traits, we can either drown them – that is, destroy them by force of will – or teach them to swim by using them creatively. Thérèse often chose the latter course.

Although the mature Thérèse sincerely desired to be forgotten, the child was fond of the limelight. She enjoyed shining at catechism, she delighted in praying aloud on behalf of the first communicants, she loved reciting poems at home and telling stories to a playground audience. She was mistress of ceremonies at bird funerals and she was probably chief hermit when she played solitaries with her cousin Marie Guérin. Even as a very small child, she announced that she would be the reverend mother in a convent.

Thérèse never lost her love of the limelight but she "taught it to swim" as part of her mature personality. After all, she chose what was the fiercest limelight of all: sanctity. Of course she realised that to be a saint she must forget herself. So the love of the limelight gradually became a desire to carry within herself the true light that is most perfectly enhanced by vessels of earthenware. She would seek the glory of God and abandon her own glory to him.

Still adopting the creative approach, Thérèse taught even her scruples to swim! That is, she took her tendency to agonise over minutiae and transformed it into an awareness of the importance of little things. God may not be concerned with a heap of trifles but he is pleased, Thérèse believed, by trifling acts of unselfishness, little gestures of kindness, small glances of love and trust.

Another trait that Thérèse transformed rather than lost,

was her obstinacy. Zélie Martin described her youngest child as "almost invincibly obstinate". Now the obstinacy that we deplore is merely the obverse of the perseverance that we admire. So Thérèse changed from a mulish infant into a determined young girl who promised never to be discouraged and stubbornly refused to aim at anything less than perfection. She had not lost her native obstinacy, merely channelled it to good effect.

As an infant, Thérèse was impatient. She never really lost that trait either. But whereas the child was impatient to get her own way, the adult was impatient to arrive at her goal of sanctity. This holy impatience is clearly present when she tells her novices that those who are *hurrying along the way of love* should not worry about possible future suffering. That would be to meddle in God's creative work. Thérèse took care never to interfere with God's creative work in her life or in the lives of those entrusted to her care. Rather, she took everything that God sent her and used it in co-operation with him.

Here we come to the mainspring of Thérèse's creativity: she was a "co-worker with God himself". [1] To work with God, to align herself with God's creative plan for her life, this was much more to Thérèse than success in any of the things we usually classify as "creative". Poetry, painting, writing – all these activities pale beside the central task of fulfilling God's will. Holiness, she reminds us, consists in doing God's will, being what he wants us to be. According to Léon Bloy, the only tragedy is not to have been a saint. Thérèse would have endorsed that.

All creativity originates with the God whose Spirit moved over the waters of chaos, bringing light and life out of the darkness. And the saints are those who allow this same Spirit to bring order out of the chaos of their lives. For our lives are indeed chaotic without the gentle moulding of the hands of God. Whether we acknowledge it or not, it is God who gives us meaning and direction. To be a saint is to realise this truth and to rejoice in it. To be a saint is to work with the Creator as he shapes us to the full stature of Christ. Thérèse was a saint who understood this and who desired all her little souls to live creatively, shaped by the divine hands, growing into the fullness of love.

7

Contentment

> The quality of our contentment is a measure whereby we
> may judge whether we really know God.
>
> *J.I. Packer*
>
> Everything that happens is adorable.
>
> *Léon Bloy*

The wise priest who prepared our class for confirmation used to say, "Don't be one of the *if-only-ers* of life! If only I had this, if only I were that... if only I had done something different!"

At the end of her life, Thérèse was asked what she would do if she had her time over again. "Exactly the same", she replied. That is surely the answer of a contented person, a very unusual person; most of us would like to make more than a few modifications to our life-story!

At first sight, it seems as if Thérèse were somewhat self-satisfied, lacking that "divine discontent" which spurs us on to progress and achievement. However, if we follow the contentment curve in Thérèse's life, we shall get a different impression. Thérèse's contentment on her deathbed was the contentment of surrender and total abandonment to God. It was in fact the virtue of contentment.

Now contentment as a virtue is very different from the images we usually associate with the word. "Contentment" evokes pictures of a cat curled up in front of the fire, a sleeping child, someone in a deck chair on a sunny day, a dog at its master's feet. All these images are static whereas the virtue of contentment is dynamic because it means keeping pace with God. It means being happy with all he sends us. "It is what he does that I like", asserts Thérèse.

How did Thérèse attain such a plateau of serenity? Not without many struggles and disappointments. So, if we too desire to acquire the virtue of contentment, we should follow her progress and learn from her example.

Like all children, the small Thérèse was contented and discontented by turns. When things went her way, she smiled and laughed; when anything thwarted her, she howled and raged. One would hardly expect anything else from a small child. Gradually, however, Thérèse learned the concept of sacrifice, overcoming herself in small ways in order to please God. The centre of her contentment began to shift; no longer was it entirely related to her own wellbeing. There were other people to consider, too. Pleasing God meant pleasing one's family and friends by loving and unselfish behaviour.

Now there is always an element of discontent in the growing child, it would be unnatural and wrong were it otherwise. A child is right to be discontented with its low stature and limited abilities. It needs to aspire to greater things if it is to mature. It needs to look forward to "when I grow up", it needs to dream of being a nurse or a ballet dancer or an engine driver. Thérèse certainly had a sizeable "if only" element in her make-up. If only she were a little taller ("just the height of a stool", teased Céline), then she would be her elder sister's confidante. If only she hadn't been born on 2nd January, she would have made her first communion a whole year earlier. If only she didn't have to go to school. If only she could overcome her scruples and tearfulness!

It was the question of tearfulness that was an important turning point for Thérèse. She always regarded the final victory over her hypersensitivity, on that Christmas morning of 1886, as a small miracle. The miracle was a complete and definitive shift in her centre of contentment.

She says that she forgot herself in order to please others and from then on she was happy. The child, who had hitherto been seeking her own contentment, began actively to seek that of others. This is not to say that Thérèse had been a completely selfish child, merely that she had been sorely hampered by her hypersensitivity and there is always an element of selfishness in the over-sensitive. It is not necessarily culpable; it is simply a matter of failing to get one's priorities right. For the over-sensitive person is one who refers all events to self first and only secondly to others. Now Thérèse got the order right: God, others, self. It was an order she was to maintain all her life. However, she had still a long way to go before achieving perfect contentment.

Saint Paul tells us, "I have learned in whatsoever state I am, therewith to be content." [1] Thérèse also had to learn to be content. She learned it in some twenty years. Most of us take a bit longer, so we can usefully consider her methods. To be content means to be contained within the limits of one's desires. The opposite state, discontent, is neatly summed up by Shelley: "We look before and after and pine for what is not."

Thérèse as a young girl was much given to "looking before and after", especially at the time of her scruples when her eyes were constantly fixed on her imaginary wrongdoings. She also pined for what was not: she wanted to be a nun and a great saint and neither goal seemed to be within reach.

After Thérèse had been cured of her scruples, she felt a great peace but she would not be content until she had succeeded in storming the gates of Carmel and even then there was the question of that seemingly unattainable sanctity.

Thérèse learned valuable lessons about contentment on her pilgrimage to Rome. She had pinned all her hopes on a favourable response from the Holy Father to her request to enter Carmel at the age of fifteen. "You will enter if the good Lord wills" the Pope had told her. At that moment, it looked as if it was not God's will and Thérèse tearfully struggled to accept this. Pauline wrote from Carmel to console her and it was to an image of Pauline's that Thérèse had recourse: the image of the little ball. Thérèse pictured herself as a little ball, a cheap toy offered to the Child Jesus. He was free to play with it, reject it or even pierce a hole in it to examine the contents. This sentimental image conceals a demanding reality; it is hard to accept that one is a cheap plaything in the hands of a capricious infant. The aim of her pilgrimage seemed to have failed but she says she was at peace. She had done all she could to follow what she believed was God's will and she began to find contentment in abandoning her future to God. She echoed in her heart the divine intention, "See, I come... I am content to do your will, O my God."[2]

Once Thérèse had entered Carmel, there were further lessons to be learned. After the initial delight at being in the "desert" of Carmel, Thérèse, as we have seen, was dismayed at the behaviour of some of the other desert-dwellers! There was the prioress, so kind and encouraging before Thérèse's entry, now so severe to her Teresita. There were one or two neurotic nuns and several very difficult ones. Thérèse says feelingly that one would go a long way round to avoid meeting them!

The sense of disappointment on entering a convent is almost universal. True, there are souls like St Elizabeth of the Trinity who seem to have found their new homes well nigh perfect, but the opposite reaction is more common. Most postulants have very rosy expectations of their companions in religion and are consequently disappointed to find them all too human.

At first, Thérèse must have found it difficult not to be discontented. Was this mount Carmel and these her fellow climbers? She noted a certain laxity in keeping the rule and often longed to correct those whom she saw at fault. In this, Thérèse was like every young person of high ideals: she wanted to set the world to rights. Gradually, however, she began to incline to the attitude of St Teresa who advised, "Let us take note of our own shortcomings and leave other people's alone. Those who live carefully regulated lives are disposed to be shocked at everything, whereas we could learn important lessons from the very persons who shock us. Our outward comportment and behaviour is perhaps superior to theirs but even if this matters, it is not what matters most."[3]

Thérèse began to understand that what mattered most was to obey Christ's command to love others as he loved them. How, she wondered, did Christ love us? Surely by encouraging our least signs of virtue, by enduring our repeated failures.

It was through her own repeated failures that Thérèse learned tolerance of others' faults. She learned to achieve contentment with regard both to herself and others when she realised the endless patience of God towards us. She would doubtless have endorsed Don Augustin Guillerand's wise dictum,

"Follow grace in souls; take its step. It is *adagio,* often *adagissimo.*"[4]

Although Thérèse acknowledged these truths, there still remained an area of unfulfilled desire in her heart. She admitted that such discontent was unreasonable. To be a spouse of Christ, a Carmelite, a mother of souls, surely that should have been enough to content her but it was not! She felt in her heart other vocations: warrior, priest, apostle, doctor, martyr; she wanted to carry out the most heroic works for Jesus and she would not rest content until she had done so.

We have seen how Thérèse found the answer to the question of her vocation: she would be love in the heart of the Church. She describes how she came to this realisation:

"As Magdalene, stooping over the empty tomb, finally found what she was seeking, I bent low over the depths of my nothingness and rose so high that I was able to reach my goal."

The first half of this striking image is from the Gospel of St John, the second from a poem of St John of the Cross. The image is of a type dear to Thérèse, combining acknowledgement of her nothingness with high ambition. For the ambition to be love in the heart of the Church is high indeed; how can anyone except God *be* love? However, Thérèse has a logic of her own, in the light of which this ambition is perfectly reasonable.

Thérèse had a great affection for Mary Magdalene, the saint who had been forgiven much and therefore loved much. Thérèse herself felt that she had been forgiven, not much but everything, because God had removed stumbling blocks from her path and preserved her from mortal sin. Grateful for God's prevenient grace, she would also love much. As Magdalene bent low over the tomb, so Thérèse would bend low over the depths of her nothingness, her inability to perform heroic deeds, and so rise high enough to attain her goal. The strength to do this came from God alone. Thérèse saw that her multiple vocations would be fulfilled only if she became a little child. It was as a little child, weak and powerless, able only to love and trust her heavenly father, that Thérèse would be love. Dazzling exploits were denied her; she could not preach the Gospel or shed her blood but she could stay next to God's throne and love on behalf of her active brothers and sisters. It was only thus that she could become a saint. "I will be love, I will be a saint", it was all one.

Once Thérèse had discovered her vocation to be love in the heart of the Church, her contentment grew. All her desires had been fulfilled. Now she had only one desire: to do the will of God.

The will of God was to lead Thérèse into deepest darkness. She clung to God in the night, making more acts of faith in her last year that in all the rest of her life. Yet, because she had mastered the art of contentment, she was able to say that she was always happy and contented. She *liked whatever God did*. She was content to "sit at the table of sinners", eating the bitter bread of unbelief. She was happy to do so until God ordained it otherwise. It was a trial that was to last until her dying moments.

On her sickbed, Thérèse remained calm and contented. She said in a letter to a relative that she was as "merry as a cricket", adding that she would not be so cheerful if God had not shown her that the only joy on earth was to accomplish his will.

Again and again, Thérèse returned to this teaching: to be contented one must do God's will. She told her novices that their faces should show the contentment of happy children. She exhorted her own sisters to be content with the circumstances of her death. They must let God have his way; if she died in the night, alone, they were not to worry; her heavenly father would simply have come to fetch her.

In all this, Thérèse strove to lift the idea of contentment from the level of mere self-fulfilment and to insert it into the dynamic of Christ who always did the will of his father and was content to do it. Our notions of contentment are usually far too narrow. God is calling us into the "wide room"[5] of his eternal purposes. If we listen to her teaching and follow her example, Thérèse will be our guide.

8

Thérèse and Friendship

> For there is no friend like a sister,
> In calm or stormy weather;
> To cheer one on the tedious way,
> To fetch one if one goes astray,
> To lift one if one totters down,
> To strengthen whilst one stands.
>
> *Christina Rossetti*

> Faithful friends are life-saving medicine and those who fear
> the Lord will find them. Those who fear the Lord direct their
> friendship aright.
>
> *Ecclesiasticus 6:16-17*

Two little girls were sharing a bed. When their mother came to tuck them in, she tried to calm their fear of the dark by saying, "There's nothing to be afraid of. God is right here with you." As the door closed, a young voice spoke in the darkness, "Move over, Courtney and let God sleep in the middle."

That was admirable faith and also an excellent recipe for Christian friendship: God in the middle.

Thérèse's life illustrates this perfectly. Her friendships were God-centred and she was a wonderful friend: tender, demanding and playful by turns. However, Thérèse did not start that way. She won through to mature and balanced Christian friendship only after a painful emotional journey. We have seen how the happy, friendly infant Thérèse changed, on her mother's death, into a timid child who later found it almost impossible to make friends outside her family circle.

As Thérèse is now a canonised saint, it is tempting to believe that her friendlessness was undeserved. But saints are not born with haloes; they grow into sanctity and Thérèse was no exception. Sometimes one can understand only too well why Thérèse's schoolmates found her difficult to like. She was a conscientious student, so they probably thought of her as a "goody-goody". This impression was strengthened by her claim never to have broken the school silence rules. When another girl ventured to doubt this, Thérèse answered priggishly, "Marie, I *never* lie!" Not the way to endear oneself to one's schoolfellows!

Thérèse tried to make friends at school but she was unsuccessful. There was a particularly painful episode when Thérèse's sincerely felt overtures were met with casual indifference. Thérèse backed away, hurt and bewildered. Nothing in her loving home had prepared her for such treatment. She also noticed that some of the pupils made friends with one or other of the teaching nuns. But somehow Thérèse could not manage that either.

Lonely and dispirited, Thérèse would creep into the school chapel to be with Jesus. Was he not her only friend? she asked sadly. From the point of view of faith, that was an excellent attitude. As far as human relationships went, it was decidedly lacking.

When Thérèse entered Carmel at the age of fifteen, she prayed, "May creatures be nothing to me and I nothing to them but may you, Jesus, be everything."[1] The last part of her prayer was answered; Jesus was certainly everything to her. But the first part was to be somewhat modified. We should be grateful for that. If Thérèse had been a spiritual Miller of Dee ("I care for nobody, no not I, and nobody cares for me.") she could hardly have become such a friend to her many followers. And she is a wonderful friend: warm, encouraging and lovingly concerned with the details of our everyday lives.

When the postulant Thérèse vowed that human beings would not have an atom of her love, she was in fact conforming to the ideal prevalent in the religious life of her day. "Particular friendships" were forbidden and no one seemed to realise that friendships are by definition particular. Only Candide and his like can be "friends of all the world". Friendship need not be exclusive and inward-looking – what the French call an *égoisme à deux* – but it is by nature particular.

Friendship has an interesting history as far as the religious life is concerned. Pachomius fears that friendship will lead to favouritism or grumbling, while Cassian warns that it may detract from the love of God. Benedict feels that it may lead to factions. Augustine celebrates friendship in principle but warns against attachment to anything but God. They are all right. Friendship can indeed have all these undesirable by-products.

On the other hand, Aelred of Rievaulx's *Spiritual Friendship*, inspired by Cicero's *De Amicitia,* defines friendship as "agreement on matters human and divine, with charity and good will." Aelred explains that good will is a rational and voluntary choice to benefit someone, while charity is the enjoyment of natural affection towards someone. Aelred, whose one delight as a boy was "to love and be loved", goes so far as to say, "God *is* friendship and the one who abides in friendship abides in God."

Anselm prays for his friends like this,

> "So love them, you source of love, by whose command and gift I love them."[2]

Both Bernard and William of St Thierry extol friendship in the religious life. St John of the Cross does the same and St Teresa says,

> "I would advise those who practise prayer… to cultivate friendships… with others of similar interests… Charity grows when it is communicated to others and from this there result a thousand blessings."

However, despite the endorsement of these prominent spiritual guides, friendship seems to have become steadily more suspect in the context of the vowed life. This is a strange development when one considers the most important exemplar of all, the Lord Jesus Christ. It is clear from the Gospels that Jesus enjoyed close friendships. There were Peter, James and John who were privileged to share special moments of teaching, healing and divine revelation. John even seems to have been a very particular friend, the Beloved Disciple who leaned on Christ's breast at the Last Supper. And we must not forget Mary, Martha and Lazarus. Christ warns us against many of the snares of the spiritual life but never against friendship.

Thérèse naturally absorbed the monastic ideal of her time, which favoured a rather bland universal charity and frowned on anything approaching particularity. But God is never limited by our narrow human ideas. He can write straight with our crooked lines and his Spirit can gently bend our rigid views. Thérèse was always open to the guidance of God's Spirit and thus it was that her views on friendship were gradually modified.

Thérèse's attitude had changed out of all recognition by the end of her short nine years of monastic life. At first she vowed never to give creatures an atom of her love; later she is heard saying to her favourite novice, "I have a heart for you alone." Such a *volte face* seems to have only one explanation and it is summed up by that old monastic dictum, *contemplandum et imitandum.* As Thérèse contemplated God, she learned all the riches of the divine tenderness. She caught a glimpse of the exuberant, reckless love of a God who pours himself out in creation and redemption, heedless of his people's ingratitude, yearning only for a return of his generous love. In order to imitate such love, obviously one cannot tread warily, afraid to love those for whom Christ died.

Saint John of the Cross confirmed Thérèse in her newly

97

emerging attitude to friendship. He himself had had a loving friend in his great co-reformer, St Teresa. From personal experience, he writes,

> "When the love one has for a creature is a wholly spiritual affection and founded in God alone, it grows in proportion to the love of God in the soul; so the more we think of our friend the more we also think of God and desire him and the two loves grow together."

Thérèse, for her part, explains to her much-loved novice, Sr Mary of the Trinity,

> "Our hearts are made in the image of God who loves each of us as if there were no one else, so I can legitimately say that I have a heart for you alone."[3]

The French say that our friends are the relatives that we choose. Conversely, some of our relatives are the friends that we choose. This was the case with Thérèse. Marie and Pauline were more like mothers to her but Céline, the nearest sister to her in age, was a true friend. Céline had a rather difficult character and does not seem to have resembled Thérèse very closely, yet Thérèse does not hesitate to call her "the sweet echo of my soul". Céline was to become Thérèse's novice in Carmel where their friendship grew and deepened. Of course Thérèse was very careful never to show special favour to Céline and sometimes perhaps erred on the side of strictness. However, a true friend is one who is not afraid to correct us and point out our failings. "Faithful are the wounds of a friend," says the Scripture, "but the kisses of an enemy are deceitful."[4] Thérèse was never afraid to reprove those whom she loved and she never gave the deceitful kisses of flattery or unmerited praise.

Marie Guérin, Thérèse's cousin and childhood friend, was also under the tutelage of Thérèse in Carmel. Thérèse gave glowing accounts of Marie to the Guérin parents but she did not spare Marie a number of firm rebukes. The same applied to Sr Mary of the Trinity, the novice to whom Thérèse seems to have been closest of all.

In all this, Thérèse was completely in accord with her patron St Teresa of Avila who wrote:

"Their heart does not allow them to practise duplicity; if they see their friend straying from the road, or committing any faults, they will speak to her about it; they cannot allow themselves to do anything else. And if after this the loved one does not amend, they will not flatter her or hide anything from her… a person may be indifferent to all other people in the world and not worry whether they are serving God or not, since the person she has to worry about is herself. But she cannot take this attitude with her friends: nothing they do can be hidden from her, she sees the smallest mote in them."

A true friend is sometimes demanding, sometimes tender, sometimes playful. These three aspects of friendship are specially evident in Thérèse's relationship with Sr Mary of the Trinity. Thérèse certainly rebuked this charming and childlike novice but she also loved her most tenderly and, taking into account Mary's *caractère d'enfant*, she treated her accordingly. So, when Mary was oppressed by the austere atmosphere of Carmel, Thérèse sent her up to the attic to play with a spinning top. Mary was child enough to enjoy such a recreation and Thérèse assured her that she needed it!

Another instance of Thérèse's playfulness is the famous episode of the mussel shell, which lay on Thérèse's desk among her painting apparatus. One day, when the novice Mary was weeping, Thérèse seized the shell and started to collect Mary's tears as they fell. This ridiculous remedy soon restored the novice to cheerfulness. Thérèse was sympathetic towards this defect – had she not herself been an unbearably weepy adolescent? – but she was determined that Mary should overcome her fault and said, "From now on, you may weep as much as you like, as long as it is into the shell!"[5]

Another aspect of true friendship is the sharing of one's deepest feelings and aspirations. Thérèse certainly did this with Sr Mary of the Trinity. It was to Mary that she confided her dark temptations against the faith and also her premonitions of a future mission. Thérèse felt, with good reason, that Mary would understand these contrasting facets of Thérèse's character.

Perhaps Thérèse's most significant friendship in Carmel, from our point of view, was that which she enjoyed with her two priest "brothers" – Fathers Bellière and Roulland. The Martin family had longed for a son who would be a priest, maybe a missionary, but their three sons had all died in infancy. So when Pauline, then prioress, asked Thérèse to pray for and write to two missionary priests, Thérèse felt that the family ambition had been fulfilled. The correspondence with the two priests is not lengthy but it is supremely important as Thérèse expounds to them her "little doctrine" or Little Way to heaven. She writes to them with all the affection and candour of a sister, all the warmth and tenderness of a friend. "Truly, only in heaven will you know how dear you are to me," she writes to Fr Bellière, "I feel our souls are made to understand each other."[6]

Father Bellière seems to have been the more needy of the two. He was given to vacillation and self-doubt but he had a staunch supporter in Thérèse. She advised and encouraged him, ready to sympathise with his weaknesses and believing him capable of great things. This beautiful passage, said to originate in Arabia, would probably have described his feelings towards the young Carmelite who had so providentially become his mentor:

> "Oh the comfort, the inexpressible comfort of feeling safe with a friend, having neither to weigh thoughts nor measure words but pour them all right out just as they are, chaff and grain together, knowing that a faithful hand will take and sift them, keep what is worth keeping and then with a breath of kindness blow the rest away."

Another friend whom Thérèsian commentators seldom cast in that role, was Mother Marie de Gonzague. She was, by all accounts, a difficult woman but evidently a born leader as her frequent re-election as prioress bears witness. She was also a very strong and attractive personality. Several of the nuns later confessed that they had been overly attached to her. Thérèse, too, felt that attraction but she also felt a deep compassion for one whose character often led her into grief and strife. There was the notable occasion when numerous ballots had to be cast before Mother Marie was finally elected as prioress. The new superior, quite naturally, felt hurt; no one likes to feel such a degree of hesitation on the part of the electorate! Thérèse offered Mother Marie consolation in the form of a story featuring a shepherdess (the prioress) and a little sheep (Thérèse). This sounds sentimental but it had the desired effect; the bruised feelings of the prioress were soothed and she knew that she had a loyal ally in Thérèse. This whole episode shows Thérèse crossing the border between child and friend. After Thérèse's death, Mother Marie was to rely on the heavenly intercession of the "little sheep" who had been a true friend to her in time of need.

Perhaps one of the most valuable qualities of a friend is unshockability. Thérèse possessed this to an astonishing degree, given her prim upbringing. For example, when Céline confided to Thérèse her temptations against chastity,

Thérèse, far from being shocked, remarked serenely that she had never suffered herself in that way, so she was happy to share the burden with her sister. Other novices made similar avowals to Thérèse and never met with disapproval, only tender compassion. Thérèse, with her robust good sense, always reminded her friends that even grave faults against chastity were much less serious than the least failure in love.

As we saw at the beginning, Thérèse started by a firm determination to belong to God alone, not giving an atom of her love to human beings. But gradually she realised that this was in fact a truncated view of love. God is a jealous God, certainly, and claims first place in our hearts but he is also the one who said, "As you have done it to the least of these my brothers and sisters, you have done it to me."[7]

If this applies to acts of charity, it surely applies as well to friendship.

Saint Teresa, pondering on these truths, came to this conclusion:

> "O my Jesus, how great is the love that you have for the children of earth! The greatest service that we can render you is to leave you for love of them and for their advantage. By doing this we possess you more completely... They who do not love their friends do not love you, my Lord, for in all the blood you shed we see the exceeding great love which you bear for the children of Adam."

This was also Thérèse's conclusion: to love God, to love one's friend, it is all one. Human friendship, far from separating us from God, can serve to draw us ever closer to the one who is our eternal friend.

Thérèse is a friend to so many because she is loving and compassionate. She has suffered from difficult personal relationships, so she can sympathise with those who suffer likewise. She has known temptation and has been near despair; she has known much bereavement and much disappointment. She is above all an approachable saint, one who has walked life's ordinary ways, endured life's common pains. We can turn to her at all times and find in her a true friend.

9

Thérèse and Mary

Mary suckled God, rocked God to sleep, prepared broth and soup for God.

Martin Luther

The more I imitate the Mother of God, the more deeply I get to know God ... Mary has taught me how to love God interiorly and also how to carry out his will in all things.

St Faustina Kowalska

It was a twentieth-century pope who asked his cardinals to write an answer to the question: Why do we ask for the prayers of the Blessed Virgin? The good prelates bent to their task and much edifying ink flowed. Yet none of them actually wrote: We pray to Mary *that we may be made worthy of the promises of Christ.*

Of course the Holy Father knew that we pray to Mary for all sorts of reasons. He was merely reminding us of the most important reason: that through God's grace we may become worthy of the promises of our Saviour.

At the foot of the Cross, Mary became the Mother of all Christians. Like the Beloved Disciple, we are invited to take her into our homes and our hearts. But it is all too easy to do this in a sub-Christian way. We can make of Mary a mere miracle-worker, a goddess or a sweet motherly figure who will shield us from the wrath of her Son. She is none of these things and the Church has always striven to keep us on the right path in this important matter. Indeed, in the days of the Catholic Index of proscribed books, several volumes were banned because of their exaggerated Mariolatry. The Documents of Vatican II include this warning:

"This Synod earnestly exhorts theologians and preachers of the divine word that in treating of the unique dignity of the Mother of God, they carefully and equally avoid the falsity of exaggeration on the one hand and the excess of narrow-mindedness on the other."[1]

The key to a right devotion to Mary lies in the Word of God. It is here that we discover Mary's obedience, her silent contemplation, her acceptance of suffering, her eagerness to lead us to Christ saying, "Do whatever he tells you."[2]

One of Mary's many titles is *Janua Coeli* (Gate of Heaven). She is the door through which Christ entered the world, the gate through which heaven came to earth. It was through her *Fiat*: "Let it be done to me according to your word", that the Word became flesh and dwelt among us. When we pray to Mary that we may be made worthy of the promises of Christ, we are asking her to help us enter, at last, the gate of heaven. We are asking to be taken up into the great stream of God's purposes. When we pray to Mary we should be aware of her role as the Mother who always leads us to the Son: through Mary to Jesus. Mary is supremely important and she lovingly watches over us but she is never an end in herself; always she points beyond herself to Christ.

Because the Gospels give us very little information about Mary and quote only a few of her words, Christian devotion has sought to fill in the gaps with miraculous infancy stories and pious myths. All too often, Mary has been made into a superwoman, a figure on a pedestal. Probably there is in many people a secret desire for such a figure. It can be comforting to think that someone is fit for a pedestal, that someone is indeed, in the words of the poet, "Our tainted nature's solitary boast". Yet we cannot have a real relationship with a pedestal-dweller. Any worthwhile relationship must be with a fully human person, one who has suffered doubt and bewilderment, sorrow and incomprehension, just as we do. If we truly desire to know Mary, we must de-mythologise her.

Thérèse is a great de-mythologiser of Mary. She once exclaimed that she would have loved to have been a priest in order to preach a sermon on Mary; just one, she felt, would have been enough. If only priests would show us the virtues we can practise, thought Thérèse. We should be able to imitate Mary, who would rather have imitation than admiration. Her life was so simple!

Those are the thoughts of the mature Thérèse. As a child she would have been more traditional in her approach.

The Martin family was devoted to Mary. All the children, even the boys, bore her name and the girls were all enrolled as Children of Mary. Thérèse especially loved May, Mary's month and would eagerly decorate the family's Marian shrine. Once when Thérèse had picked a large bunch of flowers for herself, the bouquet was promptly appropriated for Mary's altar by some interfering adult. Thérèse sighed but gave up her prize; she knew that in the Martin home, Mary came first.

This early reverence gradually became a loving familiarity, especially after Thérèse's miraculous healing at the age of ten, a cure that she always ascribed to the intercession of the Virgin. Mary, from being a distant Queen of Heaven, became for Thérèse a tender mother. Having lost her own mother so young, Thérèse found it natural to turn to the Mother of God and call her "Maman". The healing act of Mary had not been a regal command but a maternal smile. All would have been well if Thérèse had kept silent, but pressed by her sister Marie's enquiries, she divulged her secret and lost her peace. Her entourage and later the excited nuns at the Carmel, had expected something more spectacular. Thérèse admitted sheepishly that she had not noticed the colour of Mary's dress or even if she had been carrying the Christ Child. No, the Madonna had simply *smiled at her.*

Thérèse never preached her sermon on Mary; instead she has left us her poem, "Why I love you, Mary." It was in May 1897 that Thérèse had confided to Céline that she still had something to do before she died: she wanted to write a poem saying why she loved Mary.

Thérèse disliked homilies extolling the extraordinary graces of Mary. She grew weary of exclaiming "Ooh! Ah!" For Thérèse, Mary was always "more mother than queen". In order for a child to love its mother, says Thérèse, the mother must weep with it and share its sorrows. Thérèse goes on to make one of her bold affirmations: as Mary possessed Christ in her body, so do we when we receive him in Holy Communion.

Thérèse suggests that it is quite possible to imitate Mary's humble virtues: her charity in visiting Elizabeth, her praise of God in the *Magnificat*, her silence in the face of Joseph's proposed rejection, her uncomplaining acceptance of the stable at Bethlehem and the flight into Egypt, her patient searching for the twelve-year-old Jesus in Jerusalem. *Mutatis mutandis*, these are all attitudes that we can imitate in our daily lives. The search for the boy Jesus is particularly relevant to our life of prayer; so often we have to search for God in the darkness of faith.

Contemplating Mary's sufferings, Thérèse wonders if it is a good thing to suffer on earth and concludes that to suffer out of love is the purest happiness. We should not forget that when Thérèse wrote that poem, she was in the deep night of faith that was to last until her death. In typically familiar manner, Thérèse tells Mary,

"Tell him not to bother about me…
He can hide himself, I consent to wait for him
Until the endless day when my faith will be
extinguished."[3]

Thérèse then turns to the ordinariness of Mary's life with its absence of raptures, miracles and ecstasies. It was by the common way that Mary journeyed to heaven. And Mary was content to be on the same level as the rest of Jesus' disciples; all who did the will of God, he said, were his brother and sister and mother.

Thérèse ends her poem with the poignant plea that, as Mary had smiled on her in the morning of her life, so she would smile on her in the evening.

The statue that had smiled at Thérèse was to accompany her to Carmel. It was before this statue that Thérèse knelt to entrust her autobiography to the Virgin. And sometimes when her novices were troubled and could not unburden themselves, she would take them to kneel before the same statue and tell Mary their problems. Thérèse, kneeling at the side, would then offer her own counsel and consolation.

Thérèse often repeated that Mary was "more mother than queen", a mother who is approachable, understanding and imitable. Thérèse has certainly helped many people to regard Mary in this light. However, there are some who baulk at the notion of the Mother of God as *imitable*. It seems almost to be a contradiction in terms. Yet Thérèse set herself to imitate Mary and she did it so well that the Abbé Hodierne, chaplain of Lisieux Carmel after Thérèse's death, wrote in a letter to Mother Marie of Gonzague that Thérèse was "a delightful miniature of the most holy Virgin." This was an astonishingly bold remark, especially in the religious atmosphere of the time when Mary was usually portrayed as queenly and inaccessible to anything but humble admiration on the part of the faithful. That anyone should imitate Mary to the point of being a "miniature" was surely unthinkable. But Thérèse is precisely the saint of the unthinkable. She urges us to re-think our religious attitudes and to allow God's light to flood our understanding.

How did Thérèse imitate Mary? Let us count the ways.

First of all, Thérèse sought to imitate the obedience of the one who said, "Let it be done to me according to your word." To obey is to follow God's will, not our own. Thérèse knew very well the dangers of self-will. Obstinate by nature, she felt a great need to be guided by God. Sanctity, she reminded her novices, was not a matter of saying, thinking or feeling beautiful things but of perfectly fulfilling God's will. No one finds this easy. Our will is a very precious thing, an echo of the divine omnipotence. Our will is the rudder of our life and even the saints struggle to hand over that rudder to God. For Thérèse obedience is not something weak and supine, rather it is a rampart against the assaults of self-will:

> "Obedience is my strong breastplate and the shield
> of my heart."[4]

As a religious, Thérèse made a vow of obedience. This vow is the means whereby monks and nuns seek to free themselves from slavery to self-will. In essence it is no different from the obligation of every Christian to obey God; it is just more clearly delineated. In principle, religious obey their superiors. Outsiders sometimes imagine that monastic obedience is the feeble resort of those who prefer other people to make their decisions for them. Doubtless there are a few religious who feel that way but the vast majority probably find obedience the most demanding of the vows. Thérèse certainly struggled with it at times; some orders were so unreasonable! Then she reflected that Christ, the Lord of the universe, was obedient not only to Mary and Joseph but even to his executioners. He also gave himself sacramentally into the hands of his priests, both the fervent and the lukewarm. In so doing, Christ was fulfilling his Father's will. That is the aim and object of all our obedience.

Mary fulfilled the divine will pre-eminently when she gave her consent to the Incarnation and she also did it throughout her life, in joy and sorrow, in times of understanding and perplexity. When we imitate Mary's self-surrender to God's will, we are not stopping at Mary herself but looking beyond her to Jesus, the pioneer of our faith and also of our obedience. Thérèse understood this; to obey is to forsake our own will and to be caught up into the will of God.

One of Mary's titles is co-redemptrix. This does not mean that Mary's role in the plan of salvation is more than human. It does mean that she is a "co-worker with God himself" for it was through her co-operation that the Word became flesh. Our role as co-workers with God is also to enflesh Christ, to bring him to a waiting world. Christ remains the sole Redeemer; our work and prayer are valuable only insofar as they are united to his saving action. As a Carmelite, Thérèse's work was primarily that of prayer. "Let us save souls!" she exhorts Céline in many of her letters. How did she set about this?

Thérèse tells us that she was not in the habit of offering up particular sacrifices for particular people (this is for Peter, this is for Paul). Rather, she offered her whole life and trusted God to use her individual acts as he saw fit. This must surely have been Mary's way of intercession. After all, once one has said *Fiat*, one has said everything; the rest is silence.

Silence! How we long for it sometimes and how we fear and avoid it, filling our waking moments with the hum of radios and cassettes, the clatter of computers and the chatter of conversation! Mary has been described as "a woman wrapped in silence". Her recorded words are few. She pondered in her heart the mysterious acts of God. Mary does not usually talk to us when we turn to her. Instead she embraces us with silent understanding. Sometimes she whispers, "Do as he tells you." Always she silently effaces herself and points to Christ. In all this Thérèse sought to follow Mary's example.

At first glance, Thérèse does not seem to fit the pattern

of a silent saint. She certainly does not stress silence in the same way as her contemporary, St Elizabeth of the Trinity. However, silence played an important role both in Thérèse's childhood and in her life as a nun.

As a small child, Thérèse was lively and precociously intelligent. She recited poems and chattered happily to her family. As we have seen, the happy infant changed dramatically after her mother's death and Thérèse became nervous and tearful. Silence assumed a greater role in her life. There was the numb silence of bereavement and the peaceful silence of the little girl who hid behind the bed curtains to "think about God." There was the silence of the fishing expeditions with Papa when she sat wrapped in meditation on the riverbank. There was the priggish silence of the child who never broke the school rule that forbade talking in the corridors. There was the silence of the forlorn schoolgirl who crept up to the chapel to pray until her father fetched her home at the end of the school day. Perhaps the most significant was the silence that Thérèse observed when wrongly accused. She preferred to keep silent rather than make excuses, recounts Thérèse in *The Story of a Soul*. Thérèse drew strength from Mary's example; the Virgin did not explain the mystery of the Incarnation to Joseph but waited for God to enlighten her spouse; the mother of God was silent at the foot of the Cross.

Perhaps the most important way in which Thérèse imitated Mary was the way of spiritual motherhood. As Pope Pius XII wrote in his encyclical *Mystici Corporis*, "Upon the mystical Body of Christ, born of the Saviour's pierced heart, Mary bestowed the same motherly care and fervent love with which she fostered and nurtured the suckling child Jesus." At Calvary, Mary received her commission as mother of souls. It is a commission shared by all intercessors.

Thérèse felt very early the call to bring forth souls for God. She was a child of thirteen when she prayed for the conversion of the murderer Pranzini. Later, when Thérèse observed the somewhat worldly clerics on the diocesan pilgrimage to Rome, she resolved to include priests among her spiritual children. Before the pilgrimage, she had naively assumed that all priests had souls "as clear as crystal"; why on earth, she wondered, did Carmel pray for priests? Now she knew; they were in just as much need as all the other fallen children of Eve! In Carmel, she offered her last communion for the conversion of Hyacinthe Loyson, a renegade Carmelite priest. One of her greatest joys in Carmel was the motherly interest she took in two missionary priests to whom she wrote and for whom she prayed constantly. We owe those two priests a great debt for it was in her letters to them that Thérèse expounded some of the most important themes of her Little Way.

As assistant novice mistress in Carmel, Thérèse became a spiritual mother to the souls under her care. If only they knew the perfection she dreamed of for their souls! Her soul would have resonated to St Paul's words, "How I am in travail until Christ is formed in you!"[5]

Travail! That was a word which Thérèse understood very well. She understood that souls are not cheap for they cost the lifeblood of Christ. Those who are united to Christ's redeeming work also share his travail. It is as if the life-giving stream of salvation rushes through their own souls and thence to the souls for whom they pray. First, as many mystics have taught, Christ must be born in our own souls; when he has come to birth in us, we can present him to a suffering world.

Like Mary on Calvary, Thérèse gave birth to Christ in darkness and pain. Like Mary, Thérèse lived in the light of the Resurrection and drew a multitude of souls in her wake. Thérèse is the saint of the Little Way. Little but not easy, it is the way of the Cross. At the end of her life, Thérèse was to walk the crucifying way of desolation and spiritual anguish. It is to this that we now turn.

10
Duel with Darkness

You must weep for me for my sins because I have no tears
and pray with me for my soul because I have no faith. You
will see fearful shapes in the darkness and wicked voices will
whisper in your ear but they will not harm you, for against
the purity of a little child the powers of Hell cannot prevail.

Oscar Wilde

Let us believe for those who do not believe, let us hope for
those who have no hope, let us love for those who cannot
love and do not know how to love – they are legion.

A Carthusian

Thérèse is a cheerful saint. Pilgrims to Lisieux will see her
face smiling on countless pious souvenirs. Even when she
carries a crucifix, the cross is swathed in roses and above it
she smiles. The Thérèse of popular piety is gentle, sweet
and slightly soppy! Sometimes it is difficult to break away
from this cloying atmosphere and to discover her true face.

Pilgrims and devotees are not the only ones to have
misunderstood Thérèse. One of the Carmelites remarked
one day in the infirmary, "They say you have never suffered
very much."

Thérèse smiled and pointed to a glass containing a
particularly unpleasant medicine that looked like some
delicious syrup. That, commented the invalid, was a picture
of her life; people had always imagined her drinking
exquisite liqueurs while in fact there had been much
bitterness. But no, she corrected herself; her life had not
been bitter because she had known how to find joy and
sweetness in all her hardships.

Once more, this is the mature Thérèse speaking. She

had indeed discovered the "Christian's stone" which turns the base metal of trials into the gold of joyful conformity with God's will, but it had not always been so. Thérèse had to struggle for many years before attaining peace in the heart of conflict and joy in the midst of pain.

It is astonishing that anyone who knew Thérèse could have supposed that her life had been free from suffering. The briefest glance at her childhood will dispel any such illusion.

As an infant Thérèse's life had been saved by a wet nurse but the price had been high. At the age of fifteen months, the child who had grown up in a rough but cheerful country cottage was suddenly transported to a town house in Alençon where everything, including her parents and siblings, was distressingly unfamiliar: no more sweet-smelling hayfields, no more rides on the family cow and, worst of all, no more Rose, the sturdy peasant woman whom she had known as mother. Thérèse reaction was that of any bereft infant: she protested loudly.

Thérèse gradually settled back into her own family and remembered her infancy as a time of happiness. But worse bereavement was to come; Zélie died when Thérèse was only four-and-a-half years old. This time, Thérèse recalls, she did not weep much. She suffered, as many young children suffer, mutely and uncomprehendingly. Perhaps none of us comprehends suffering but adults can at least verbalise their anguish and share it with others. The small child, lacking the tools of words, can often fall into a despairing silence. The wound is not thereby healed but merely covered over; any similar suffering in later life will cause it to throb painfully. That is what happened to Thérèse who was to lose two substitute mothers, Pauline and Marie, during her childhood. The first loss was the worst. Pauline had acted as a loving mother to Thérèse and the prospect of life without her was grim indeed. So grim did it seem that Thérèse soon fell seriously ill. Even when she had been physically healed by the Virgin's smile, Thérèse remained emotionally fragile for three more years. It was not until 1886, two years before her entry into Carmel, that Thérèse began to defy and finally to conquer the darkness in her life.

Thérèse's first conquest was over her scruples. It is no use reasoning with scrupulous people; only a strong infusion of grace can cure them. In the midst of her misery, Thérèse realised this and that is why she asked the help of her dead brothers and sisters. Later in life, she was to remember her youthful conflicts and was able to console others similarly afflicted. For example, her cousin Marie Guérin was extremely scrupulous and wanted to abstain from communion on account of her supposed sins. Thérèse pointed out that such conduct was playing into the hands of the devil who would be delighted to deprive us of grace. God was much better than Marie imagined, said Thérèse. The only cure was to receive grace and the greatest grace lay in communion with the God who loved us and longed to heal us.

The most definitive conquest was yet to come: Thérèse's "complete conversion" on 25 December 1886. This event marks the beginning of a new period in Thérèse's life, a period of light and growth.

It was such an apparently small event: a weepy young girl controls her tears and begins to think of pleasing others! Perhaps it would have remained a small event if Thérèse had not realised its full significance. But Thérèse was well aware that something momentous had happened to her: she had emerged from the gloom of self-pity, which has been rightly dubbed "the shroud of the soul".

Like the apostles, Thérèse felt that she had been fishing in the dark and catching nothing. She had struggled in vain for ten long years against her hypersensitivity. Then at the midnight Mass of Christmas 1886, the light of the infant Christ flooded her soul. The night of weakness was over and shortly afterwards the strong love of a redeeming God led Thérèse to realise her vocation as "fisher of souls". Thérèse, emerging from her personal darkness, had been given new eyes to see religious truths afresh. Thus, when looking at a familiar picture of the crucified Christ, Thérèse was struck by the blood that fell from the divine hands with no one to gather it up. Thérèse immediately resolved to stand in spirit at the foot of the Cross; she would gather the precious blood and pour it over needy souls. She understood that Jesus' cry "I thirst!" was a cry not only for water but also for souls. Thérèse would quench that thirst by giving him souls.

Thérèse, never one to do things by halves, decided to pray for great sinners. It was typical of her new boldness that she chose the hardened criminal Pranzini for her first "client".

From that time on, Thérèse was to exercise her ministry of intercession, her "fishing for souls", in a variety of ways. Always she would seek in her prayer to shine the light of God's redeeming love into lives that had become overshadowed by sin and shame.

In 1887, the year following Thérèse's conversion, Louis, Céline and Thérèse set off on their pilgrimage to Rome. As we have seen, it was during that journey that Thérèse began to understand the Carmelite custom of praying specially for the priesthood. Priests were light-bearers, bringing the good news of salvation to a world darkened by sin. If their light were to grow dim, how could they fulfil their high calling?

Once arrived in Carmel, Thérèse had various types of "darkness" to face. There was the severity of a hitherto kindly Mother Marie de Gonzague. There were also petty jealousies, lack of discipline, failures in charity. Thérèse assures us that she suffered from none of the "illusions of the early days" but sometimes the low standard of general behaviour must have been daunting.

Thérèse bore all this with courage and faith. She was far from believing herself perfect so why should she expect perfection in others? Undiscouraged, she kept her eyes off the darkness of sin and failure and on Christ, the Light of the world. She began to understand that light and darkness, good and evil, are intermingled in every soul. If we let him, Christ will finally triumph over our darkness. Meanwhile, God is able to use both the good and the evil that he finds within us. He who wrested life out of primeval chaos is certainly able to create order in our turbulent hearts.

A much deeper darkness fell on Thérèse and all the Martin sisters as a result of Louis' mental illness and confinement in the home of the Bon Sauveur at Caen. Thérèse had always regarded her father as a saint; his family and friends had held him in high esteem. As her uncle Guérin used to say, "We are pygmies beside that man!" Now Louis was humiliated and diminished.

Thérèse and her sisters suffered deeply from the lack of understanding shown by some of the Carmelites and by various acquaintances outside the order. Like Job, Louis was despised because of his misfortune. His reputation was tarnished. God had touched him.[1]

Out of this darkness, Thérèse triumphantly brought light. It was the dark light of faith, however. Before this, she had asked God for suffering, now she admitted that she could bear no more. It was in the midst of the darkness that she developed and deepened her meditation on the Holy Face.

As Thérèse pondered on the Holy Face, she realised the extent of Christ's identification with the pain and humiliation of suffering humanity. She saw in Louis' humiliation a reflection of the Suffering Servant, the one who "was despised and we did not esteem him"[2] Thérèse looked beyond the darkness of the Cross to the light of the Resurrection. Louis, the faithful follower of the Suffering Servant, would certainly be placed among the saints: "I will divide him a portion among the great and he shall divide the spoil with the mighty."[3] Darkness would give way to light, Thérèse was sure of it. She knew that her beloved father would pass from his tribulation to a joyful resurrection. And when Louis finally died, Thérèse could rejoice and say with characteristic boldness, "Our father who is in heaven."

Although Thérèse suffered deeply with Louis, she never lost sight of the end of the journey: heaven. However, when she herself was faced with mortal illness, she was also faced with a prolonged trial of her faith. The luminous certainty of heaven vanished overnight, leaving her in a dark tunnel. She believed that the tunnel led upwards to the top of the mountain of Love, but she could see nothing, feel nothing but an agony of doubt.

It all started with Thérèse's first blood-spitting in the early hours of Good Friday, 1896. Far from being alarmed, she was excited at this first sign of the approach of the Bridegroom. She speaks of gaiety, fervour, consolation. But soon after Easter Thérèse was plunged into spiritual darkness. It is interesting that Thérèse should compare this darkness with the "lively faith" she had hitherto enjoyed, for she had in fact suffered from almost continual aridity since her first days in Carmel. Clearly that aridity, with its lack of sensible consolation, was of a very different order from the blackness in which she now found herself. She struggles to describe it: a shadowy tunnel, a foggy country, a black hole. She hears the mocking voice of unbelievers, inviting her to rejoice in her approaching death, which will bring her, not what she hopes for, but the darker night of nothingness.

Thérèse tells us that heaven, the goal of all her striving, had become for her a subject of conflict and torment. This has caused some commentators to speak of Thérèse's atheism. However, Thérèse's conflict seems to have centred, not on her belief in God, but on her belief in heaven. Her darkness strengthened rather than weakened her belief in God. She tells us that when she is tempted not to believe in heaven, she *runs to Jesus*; that is hardly the behaviour of an atheist. She tells Jesus that she is ready to shed her last drop of blood to affirm that heaven exists. She adds that she is happy, while on earth, not to enjoy a belief in heaven, if through her suffering she may win the gift of faith for unbelievers.

Thérèse experiences at first hand the feelings of the unbeliever. Although, it is true, she still believes in God, she feels nothing. In a desolate moment, she compares her faith-filled poems with the darkness of her soul, saying that when she sings of the joy of heaven, she feels no joy at all because she is singing simply of what she *wants to believe.*

"I want to believe!" There are many people today who experience the same longing. Gone are the days of widely held faith, gone are many of the consoling supports of religion. Of course the Church still stands like a loving mother to welcome and comfort her children but the children are very often unaware of her; they have forgotten their way back home. And the Church herself is invaded by schism and unbelief, racked by scandals and controversy. This is nothing new; the Church has suffered internal conflict from the time when the apostles argued about who would be the greatest. However, unbelief is more widespread at the beginning of the twenty-first century than it was at the time of Thérèse's death in the 1890's and Thérèse's anguish finds an echo in many hearts today. Across the years, she reaches out to all who are afflicted by unbelief and she walks courageously through the night, holding all her fellow-sufferers in her heart.

"I have come to pray for souls and especially for priests", Thérèse had declared at her examination before making her religious vows in 1890. Her long trial of faith became her supreme opportunity to practise this resolution.

For Thérèse, as for all intercessors, prayer is not merely

a matter of words, a making of intentions or a reading of lists of names. True intercession is putting one's life on the line. Christ, the perfect intercessor, said, "I lay down my life."[4] Jesus gave his life for the salvation of the world but this supreme surrender was not made in isolation. Rather, it was the culmination of a whole life of conformity to God's will. Christian intercession follows the same pattern. Intercessory prayer is not an attempt to influence God but a surrender to God's will; thus we become channels for God's grace in the lives of those for whom we pray.

It was in this atmosphere of loving surrender that Thérèse prayed for all who, like her, shared the anguish of unbelief. Abandoning herself to the will of God, she accepted her darkness and believed that her acts of faith and love would bring light to all those who walked in night.

Thérèse uses various images to describe and also to make sense of her predicament. She imagines that she was born in a fog-bound land where she had never seen sunlight; her true country, a land of brilliant sunshine, lies elsewhere. She knows that this is no myth invented by an inhabitant of her desolate native land for the king from the sunlit country had spent thirty-three years in the shadowy land of her birth. The darkness did not understand that this king was the Light of the world but Thérèse understood and she was willing to sit at the "table of sinners", eating the bitter bread of unbelief, trusting that one loving soul might purify and enlighten that place of woe, praying that the light of faith might finally shine in the hearts of her suffering brothers and sisters.

If Thérèse speaks of "poor sinners" as if she were different from them, it is not to show her own superiority. Plunged in such frightening darkness, she is far from feeling herself superior to anyone. Yet she is different in one important respect: she possesses the gift of faith. Far from priding herself on this, she realises that it is indeed a gift. That she has seen the light of the Gospel from her earliest days is due to no merit of her own. And because she has received this gift she must use it, even in the agony of apparent abandonment by God. She echoes Christ's desolate cry, "My God, my God, why?" and like Christ she wrests light from the deepest darkness and she repeats the words which had inspired her from childhood, "Even if he slays me, yet I will trust him."[5]

Christ in the Garden and on the Cross experienced utter dereliction and felt abandoned by his Father. This is a mystery both profound and consoling. How could God be separated from God? How could the ever-obedient Son suffer such desolation? His was the agony, ours the consolation of knowing that, however deep our sense of loneliness, Christ has shared it with us and for us. Thérèse, by sharing Christ's desolation, also shares in the saving work of the one who "poured out his soul unto death... and bore the sins of many and made intercession for the transgressors."[6] To share in Christ's saving work, to follow him in the darkness of dereliction, this is true intercession.

To share in Christ's saving work is indeed a high honour but it is nonetheless painful. Thérèse was always telling her novices that it was an illusion to want to suffer nobly. Christ on the Cross, suffered in desolation and died in agony yet his death was the most beautiful the world has ever known. In order to please God in our suffering, says Thérèse, we do not need to be noble, we simply have to accept his will peacefully.

In her suffering, as in every other aspect of her life, Thérèse strove to avoid the extraordinary. She was content to suffer humbly and quietly. She likens herself to a little bird drenched by a storm. The dark skies hide the sun and the bird shivers in the downpour, yet it knows that beyond the clouds the sun is shining. This is a typical Thérèsian image: the apparent sentimentality of a dear little bird caught in the rain, hides the profoundly demanding reality of faith exercised in darkness and abandonment.

We should be deeply thankful that Thérèse suffered in such an unpretentious way. It means that we can imitate her. She has passed through the darkness of both spiritual and physical suffering, not in the manner of a bold knight on a white horse but with the humble simplicity of a little child. She has shown us that against the purity of childhood, the simple trust of the infant who abandons herself to her father's arms, the powers of hell cannot prevail. This does not mean that we shall cease from suffering, that we shall stop straining to see some ray of comforting light. Thérèse herself endured spiritual darkness with scant alleviation, until the last moment of her life. Like her, we can rely on God our sun who shines beyond the darkness, who has compassion on our weakness and will draw us in the end into his everlasting light.

11
Empty Hands

> Nothing in my hand I bring,
> Simply to thy Cross I cling.
>
> *A.M. Toplady*

In June 1895, just over two years before her death, Thérèse completed her Offering to Merciful Love in which she says that in the evening of her life, she will appear before God with empty hands, for she does not ask him to count her works, for all our righteousness is tainted in his sight. So she wants to be clothed in his own righteousness.

Empty hands are the hands of the poor and Thérèse is the poorest of saints. True, she is not poor after the manner of the mendicant Francis nor is she destitute like St Benedict Joseph Labre. But she is poor in the most fundamental sense: "nothing clings to my hands", she says. Even her virtues are not her own; they are on loan from God. It is the Lord who has done great things for her; her only contribution has been her poverty.

As a nun Thérèse professed the three evangelical counsels of Obedience, Chastity and Poverty. Obedience aims to free us from self-will, chastity from the tyranny of the flesh, poverty from attachment to this world's goods. All Christians are called to live some form of the counsels; we must all obey God, live chastely and avoid covetousness and greed. Religious vows are but one way of doing this. All three counsels are in direct imitation of the Christ who was poor, chaste and obedient during his earthly life. Poverty, however, is the one counsel that has a more extensive meaning because it pertains to the very essence of God. We worship the Son who, "though he was rich yet became poor".[1] We acknowledge his presence under the poor and humble signs of bread and wine. And we believe in the radical poverty of the holy Trinity, each Person being utterly given to the others in an ecstasy of perfect love. God gives himself totally therefore he is totally poor. It is against this background that we can fully comprehend the riches of poverty.

The observance of poverty varies greatly among the religious orders and among individual houses. Sometimes the houses are in fact wealthy and their poverty is somewhat contrived. This usually means that although the house is not poor, the individual religious do not have personal possessions; they live, as did the early Church, with all things in common.

The observance of poverty at Lisieux Carmel was not a problem: they really were poor. And Thérèse certainly suffered from the cold as the Carmelite rule at that time permitted only one heated room in the entire house. The cells and cloisters and workrooms were all icy in the winter.

Thérèse threw herself wholeheartedly into the outward observance of poverty but she soon realised that religious poverty was not merely a matter of lacking material goods. Outward poverty was the husk; the kernel was poverty of spirit, the attitude of one who receives everything from God.

Thérèse did not learn this all at once. As a child, she had lived in a comfortable home. As a child she had been ambitious. True, her ambitions had been mostly spiritual: she was going to be a saint! – Not just any saint, mind you, but a *great saint*. It was imbued with this lofty aim that she had eagerly crossed the threshold of Carmel shortly after her fifteenth birthday.

Thérèse assures us that she was free from the "illusions of the early days" and to some extent this is true. Pauline and Marie, the two sisters who preceded her into the cloister, had told her about the life and she had a fair idea of what to expect – no rosy spectacles for Thérèse! But the rosy ideal of conquering sanctity "at the point of the sword" was to persist for some time. It was only after repeated failures to attain her ideal that Thérèse began to learn the deep lessons of poverty. She learned them so well, in the end, that she could almost be called the saint of indigence.

When the rich young ruler of the Gospel approached Jesus and asked how one could gain eternal life, Jesus invited him to sell all his possessions. This is the invitation that comes to all prospective religious: "Go, sell all that you have and come, follow me."[2] Now the actual renunciation of worldly goods, whether easy or difficult, is but the first step. If we are to be "naked followers of the naked Christ" as St Clare suggests, a much more radical stripping awaits us.

We have already seen how Thérèse, the cherished child of the Buissonnets, suffered a severe loss of status when she entered the Carmelite novitiate. As we have seen, she was constantly rebuked by the prioress; she was nothing but a " big kid" to some of the unkinder nuns. And although she shared a work assignment with Pauline, she was no longer permitted to share her inmost thoughts with the elder sister who had been her second mother.

All this was difficult enough but Thérèse experienced a more radical poverty at the spiritual level: she simply could see no way of becoming a saint! She was a grain of sand beside the towering mountains of sanctity and she soon realised that she was destined to remain so. She confesses that she is a little soul and can do only little things. The first of these little things was simply to empty her hands.

That sounds simple enough but it is not so in fact. All of us tend to keep a firm grasp on such intangibles as our original thoughts, our dignity, our independence, our virtues. Thérèse realised that all these things represented riches. If we cling to them we can never be truly poor.

Thérèse was an original thinker; she had a gift for illustrating spiritual lessons. Sometimes other Sisters appropriated these illustrations and passed them off as their own. Thérèse kept silent, reminding herself that her inspiration came from God; it did not belong to her so why should others not use it?

As for dignity, Thérèse possessed this in plenty. Recall the episode in her infancy when her mother offered a *sou* if she would kiss the ground. Thérèse drew herself up at once, declaring that she would rather not have the *sou*. Yet in Carmel Thérèse was prepared to lose her dignity for the benefit of the novices who were free to tell her exactly what they thought of her. Céline in particular availed herself of this permission and no doubt got plenty of weighty material off her chest in the process!

Thérèse was by nature adventurous; she enjoyed blazing trails, discovering new truths. She did indeed do both these things and has left her mark on many of the attitudes of the twentieth-century Church. Yet she never struck out independently of authority. Always she was an obedient child of the Church and when she composed her Offering to Merciful Love she asked to have it approved by a theologian.

At the end of her life Thérèse remarked that she had never been able to do anything on her own. The good she had accomplished, she insisted, was merely as an instrument in God's hands. Sometimes, she points out, artists amuse themselves by using defective brushes to paint a picture. In the case of the novices, Thérèse does not see herself as even a defective brush. Rather, she is simply a child who holds out her hands to receive from God the nourishment needed for his little ones. Always she is the saint with the empty hands.

Perhaps the last thing most of us want to relinquish is our cherished store of virtues. This is natural enough. After all, a virtue is acquired by constantly repeated acts; we have worked so hard to achieve it! Thérèse does not fall into the trap of attributing her virtues to herself. When commended for her patience, she assures us that it is not hers, only lent. As for abandonment to God, well, *God* placed her there. Beauty of soul? "What beauty?" she asks. "I don't see my beauty at all; I see only the graces I've received from God. You always misunderstand me; you don't know then that I'm only a little seedling..."[3]

Throughout her life, Thérèse was gradually divested of all her riches. Her ambition to be a great saint never left her but she began to see it in a different light. No longer would she conquer sanctity at sword point; instead she would become ever smaller, ever poorer, surrendering herself to the merciful love that alone could make her a saint. To belong to Jesus, wrote Thérèse, one had to be as small as a dewdrop. How few were the souls who aspired to remain as small as that!

The monastic life has one aim: God. Everything in a monastery is directed towards that aim: surroundings, lifestyle, art and literature, all tend to focus the eyes of the soul on God alone. God becomes the riches of the monk or nun. God is the treasure hidden in the field and religious have sold everything to buy the field. God is the pearl of great price; they have sold everything in order to buy that pearl. So what happens when they lose, or seem to lose, that treasure? Thérèse was to find out.

Until the last eighteen months of her life, Thérèse had enjoyed a radiant faith. She had not been granted much consolation in prayer but her faith had nevertheless been firm and joyful. Suddenly the darkness engulfed her; the hope of heaven seemed a mockery, demonic voices bade her despair. This was the ultimate poverty. It was also the closest following of the Christ who had cried, "My God, my God, why have you forsaken me?" It was spiritual destitution of the most painful kind. It was the poverty of one who, having abandoned all for God, is apparently abandoned by God himself.

As we have seen, Thérèse embraced this final,

excruciating poverty. In one of her poems she had declared that she wished to hide herself on earth, to be last in everything. Now her wish was granted. So well hidden was her suffering that people wondered if she had ever suffered at all. What would Mother Prioress find to say about her in her obituary notice? In the eyes of the world, even in the eyes of some of her fellow nuns, she had accomplished nothing. Well, she had wanted to be a little flower, a grain of sand. She had probably not envisaged the final darkness of her inability to believe in heaven but she accepted it with courage and simplicity. She was plunged in darkness while a tempest of doubt and fear raged around her. She felt like the disciples on the storm-tossed lake but she would not wake the sleeping Christ. Instead, she would allow him to sleep undisturbed. She resolved to wait in peace until the dawn broke and her little boat reached at last the heavenly shore.

Yes, Thérèse is the saint of empty hands. She rejoiced to see herself so poor and in need of mercy on her deathbed. She was in need of mercy not because she was a great sinner but because she was helpless; she could not save herself, she could not believe as she had once believed. All she could do was to throw herself into the merciful arms of the one whom she had learnt to call "Papa le bon Dieu". She was utterly poor, dependent on others for all her bodily needs, too weak to pray, too racked by pain to sleep. Even the consolation of Holy Communion was denied her in her last weeks on account of her frequent vomiting. And she waited, she said, like a child waits for her parents to put her on a train. The parents did not come and she kept missing the train for heaven. Ah well, there would be one train she wouldn't miss!

Thérèse's great riches are her empty hands. Even her own family members in the convent were slow to believe this. Marie, for example, imagined that Thérèse's "infinite desires", such as her longing for martyrdom or her missionary zeal, constituted her value in God's sight. Thérèse herself felt that she was pleasing to God because she loved her littleness and poverty and because of her blind hope in his mercy.

Yes, that is indeed where Thérèse's riches are to be found. She is the saint whose empty hands contain the mystery of God's merciful love. It is when we are empty of good works, spiritually poor to the point of destitution, that we are able to receive God's grace and mercy. God, as Thérèse repeatedly reminded her novices, has no need of our fine deeds, our lofty thoughts, our splendid desires. He needs our empty hands, stretched out in humble acknowledgement of our poverty. And when he finds us with empty hands, he hastens to fill them with the riches of his love.

12

Universal Thérèse

> To turn water into wine and what is common into what is holy, is indeed the glory of Christianity.
>
> *F.W. Robertson*

"Everyone will love me!" exclaimed Thérèse during her last illness. Well, not quite everyone. There will doubtless always be those who miss the real Thérèse who is strong, wise and joyful, and persist in seeing her as a milksop. However, this category of persons need not detain us. Let us turn instead to the vast number who appreciate and love Thérèse.

During her lifetime, Thérèse was known to a very limited number of people: her family and a few friends, her schoolteachers and companions, one or two priests. An even smaller number of these people really understood her. She lived such a hidden life in Carmel that few of her sisters ever penetrated the sweet and gentle exterior to find the blazing fire of sanctity within. This was entirely in accord with Thérèse's own wish, expressed in a poem:

"The hidden way on earth I'll take,
Be last in all for Jesu's sake."[1]

However, Thérèse's desire to be hidden seems to have been confined to this world. As she lay in the convent infirmary, Thérèse predicted, with the clairvoyance of the dying, a very different future. She would let fall a shower of roses, she prophesied. Her own sisters wanted to know if she would watch over them from heaven. No, she would come down, promised Thérèse. She wanted to spend her heaven doing good on earth.

When some thirty people attended Thérèse's burial in the local cemetery on 4 October, 1897, it would have been difficult to foresee the magnificence of her posthumous career. Yet, in Pius XI's phrase, a "storm of glory" was very soon to break about the head of little Thérèse Martin. Twenty-eight years later, the crowd had grown to a spectacular five-hundred-thousand, thronging St Peter's Square in Rome to celebrate a newly canonised member of the heavenly court: St Thérèse of Lisieux.

Thérèse is a saint of contrasts: a little soul of great faith, a simple mind rich in wisdom, a hidden life reaching, after death, to the four corners of the earth.

Today, more than one thousand seven hundred churches are dedicated to Thérèse and more than fifty religious congregations are under her patronage. She who never left her cloister is patroness of all foreign missions alongside St Francis Xavier. Thousands of healings, both physical and spiritual, are attributed to her intercession. Jean Guitton once joked that Thérèse, far from enjoying *requiem aeternam*, seemed to be engaged in *actionem aeternam*. Thérèse had said that she counted on not being inactive in heaven.

The initial spark of the great Thérèsian conflagration was undoubtedly her autobiography, *The Story of a Soul*. Translated into sixty languages, this little book has touched millions of lives. We may well ask: Why is this? What is so appealing about Thérèse?

Perhaps the most attractive Thérèsian trait is her universality. She said of her book that there was something for everyone, except for those led by extraordinary ways. Most of us are led by ordinary ways to God, so most of us can relate to Thérèse.

Most of us do not see visions or dream dreams. We enjoy no ecstasies or special revelations. We plod along in our prayers as best we may. And then we open the writings of the one whom Pope Pius X called "the greatest saint of modern times" and we discover that she is very like us.

Thérèse's cousin, Marie Guérin, was one of those who recognised Thérèse's unassuming holiness during her lifetime. Writing some two months before Thérèse's death, she says:

> "It's not an extraordinary sanctity, with a love of extraordinary penances, no it's the love of God. Those in everyday walks of life can imitate her sanctity, for she has simply tried to do everything out of love and to accept all the little annoyances, all the little sacrifices of each moment as coming from the hand of God. She sees God in everything and does everything as perfectly as possible. And she knew how to sanctify pleasure, too, by offering it to God."[2]

This was Thérèse's Little Way: humble, simple and imitable. Simple, but not easy, it is in fact very demanding. However, Thérèse assures her followers that God will demand of them not glorious deeds but humble trust, not spiritual riches but poverty.

Thérèse promised that if she had been mistaken in her teaching, she would return to earth and warn her followers. She has indeed returned to earth, not in warning but in confirmation of her Little Way. The Church has always recognised miracles as God's "seal of approval". It is said of the apostles that when they preached the Word of God, the Lord worked with them and confirmed the word with the miracles that followed. Countless wonders have confirmed the words of Thérèse. There are miraculous healings ascribed to her intercession and many conversions. However, Thérèse does not convert all her clients. She has an enthusiastic following, for example, in Cairo where on most days one thousand five hundred worshippers, mostly Moslems, come to pray in the basilica dedicated to her. A Catholic priest, astonished at such an influx of non-

Christians, asked a Moslem why Thérèse was so popular. "It's because she listens to our prayers", came the simple reply.

Now healing and conversions are what one would expect at the intercession of a saint but Thérèse also specialises in practical aid to those who invoke her. For example, she has been known to guide a lost pilgrim to the station in Lisieux, to plead for an employee who had been sacked, even to find documents in the archives of a bank. On all these occasions, Thérèse was seen "in the flesh". Evidently her promise to spend her heaven in doing good on earth included attention to the details of daily life. This is of course in keeping with the spirit of the Little Way, the way of practical, little things.

Thérèse's miracles are certainly impressive; at Lisieux alone there are some three thousand two hundred pages recounting them. Many more doubtless go unrecorded. But her "shower of roses" is by no means confined to the visible and tangible. Outward signs and marvels, Thérèse seems to say, are not necessarily God's choicest gifts. She warned her blood sisters in Carmel not to expect special favours from her when she was in heaven. Perhaps they would have great trials, but she promised to send them lights that would make them appreciate and love them.

These trials took various forms. Marie endured long years of crippling arthritis; to Pauline fell much of the arduous work connected with Thérèse's canonisation: editing documents, preparing testimonies, answering hundreds of letters, assuming the lifelong leadership of the Lisieux Carmel. As for Céline, perhaps her greatest trial was her own intractable personality. Thérèse certainly appeared to work no miracle of transformation in the life of the one whom she had called "the sweet echo of my soul". Try as she would, Céline could not achieve the peace and humility for which she longed. All her life, she battled against her imperious nature and her quick temper.

133

Intelligent, gifted and determined, she persevered for sixty-five years in Carmel, dying at the age of ninety. When she was seventy-two, she could be heard lamenting, "I shall always be a "daughter of thunder", alas! – and the good Lord will have to take me as I am, vibrant and pugnacious."[3]

Should we conclude from this that Céline was one of Thérèse's failures? Certainly not! Céline did not achieve the perfection of which she dreamed but she probably achieved the perfection that God had in mind for her. When she came to die, God would not ask her why she had not been Thérèse but he would ask her if she had been Céline. And she could answer yes; she had lived to the full with the temperament God had given her: quick to speak, quick to repent, enthusiastic, loyal and affectionate. Perfection, Thérèse taught, consists in doing God's will, being what he wants us to be. Céline is an example and encouragement to all who struggle with a difficult personality. She is also a triumph of Thérèse's Little Way, the way of those who are aware of their utter dependence on God's grace and mercy.

Another relative to whom Thérèse seems to have shown no special favour, was her cousin Jeanne Guérin, uncle Isodore's eldest daughter. "I pray to the Servant of God", she reported, "but I notice she sends me more crosses than consolations."

If Thérèse does not always work miracles for her friends, she keeps her promise to send lights that will make them appreciate and love their trials. As she pointed out to her own sisters, she herself had not enjoyed constant miraculous deliverance from her own trials. Her autobiography recounts, instead, the sustaining grace of the God who was with her in spiritual darkness and physical pain.

Thérèse died at the end of the nineteenth century, a time of spiritual confusion for many. Christians were still suffering the influence of Jansenism: moral rigour, coupled with the image of an angry God and the consequent fear of hell. Of course Jansenism stood condemned but traces of that gloomy doctrine still persisted in the minds and hearts of the faithful and an astonishing number of nuns were mortally afraid of damnation. At the opposite pole, there was a growing tide of atheism, the foremost of whose exponents was Nietzsche, a contemporary of Thérèse. "The concept of God", he wrote, "was invented as the opposite of the concept 'life' – everything detrimental, poisonous and slanderous and all deadly hostility to life, was bound together in one horrible unit!"

"God is dead!" proclaimed Nietzsche, to which Thérèse replied with all the vehemence of her nature, "I know that my Redeemer lives!" But it is in darkness that Thérèse makes this affirmation; it is in blood that she writes her creed. It is from the depths of near despair and temptation to suicide, that Thérèse shouts her faith. She once confessed that if she had not had faith, she would have committed suicide without a moment's hesitation, such was the intensity of her physical suffering.

Thérèse is no plaster saint, standing untouched by the trials and torments of life. She is a saint who has sweated and wept. Certainly she relinquished her attempt to conquer perfection at sword point but faith, that was another matter. Faith she had to conquer blow by blow while the mocking voices of unbelief whispered in her ears.

Nietzsche wrote a series of works "whose common goal", he said "is to erect a new image and ideal of the free spirit." Of course the free spirit in the sense of the free thinker, was nothing new. A century before, a Voltaire, a Jean-Jacques Rousseau had uttered their elegant blasphemies. Unlike Nietzsche, both were deists. Voltaire, while acknowledging a rather vague Supreme Being, seems to have regarded religious belief as a mere guardian of morals: "I want my attorney, my tailor, my valet to believe in God; I imagine I am thereby less likely to be robbed."[4] Rousseau, for his part, vacillated between humble adoration: "The most noble use of my reason is to prostrate myself before you (God)" and the astonishing impertinence of "I suffice unto myself, like God."

The nineteenth century, which saw tremendous missionary expansion, was also a time of widespread agnosticism and atheism. This was Thérèse's century. In France the faith of Chateaubriand, Lamartine and Hugo compete on the literary stage with the anti-clericalism of Stendhal and Mérimée, the tortured outpourings of Baudelaire, Verlaine and Rimbaud. It was a century of much religious anguish and doubt. Many of the literary figures, while rejecting their childhood faith, nevertheless chose religious themes and agonised over religious problems such as divine justice and mercy and the role of Providence in human life. There is a certain nobility in their atheism, a certain courage in their agnosticism. They had ceased to believe but they had not ceased to struggle valiantly. So de Vigny declares,

> "To groan, to weep, to pray,
> Are but the coward's way.
> Fulfil with energy
> Your given destiny
> Face your last agony;
> In silence die, like me."[5]

And, across the Channel, some forty years later, W.E. Henley was echoing similar sentiments:

> "I thank whatever gods may be
>
> For my unconquerable soul."[6]

Thérèse had received a somewhat limited education but she was certainly familiar with some of the religious poetry of her time. She also knew of the existence of unbelievers. She admits in her autobiography that at first she could not believe in unbelief; surely the people concerned were speaking against their better judgment! She became aware of the reality of unbelief in a particularly painful way, by her involvement in the "Taxil affair."

It all started when a certain Diana Vaughan, a former Freemason, published her memoirs, in which she described her conversion to Catholicism, due to the influence of Joan of Arc. Thérèse, a great admirer of Joan, had recently written a play about the young French heroine. The young nun asked permission to write to Miss Vaughan, enclosing a photograph of herself and Céline in the roles of Joan and St Catherine, in the convent play. It was this photograph that was on display on 19 April 1897 when Diana Vaughan was booked to attend a press conference in Paris. The celebrated convert had hitherto refused to appear in public and everyone soon knew the reason. At the appointed hour, instead of a young woman, a small, stout man strode onto the stage. Meet Leo Taxil, practical joker supreme! Taxil was hustled off the stage under police protection, narrowly escaping the wrath of an outraged audience. There was consternation in Lisieux when the press reported the hoax. Thérèse, very ill by then and in the dark night of faith, was deeply humiliated. She tore up the letter she had received from "Diana Vaughan" and threw it on the manure heap. She redoubled her prayers for those who had no faith and through the abuse of grace, had lost that precious treasure.

Because Thérèse herself suffered agonies of doubt and was tempted to despair and suicide, she is close to all such sufferers. She has plunged into the gloom and walked in the darkness, singing the song of faith. It is a song that was evermore necessary, as the noble defiance of the nineteenth century's intellectuals gave way to a blacker mood in the twentieth: total disillusionment in the wake of two world wars, a slow but sure erosion of that peculiarly nineteenth century myth, the perfectibility of humankind. Science had not brought forth Utopia, man's inhumanity to man had plumbed new depths. The theatre of the absurd flourished in Europe and Osborne's character gave voice to the mood of the day: "There's nothing left to die for!" The literary scene was haunted by the spectre of meaninglessness. As Nietzsche had exclaimed at the turn of the century, "It is not so much the suffering as the senselessness of it that is unendurable."

Thérèse was well acquainted with the feeling of meaninglessness. She had struggled at intervals all her life to wrest meaning from her sufferings. There was the shattering event of her mother's death, her own serious illness in childhood, the humiliation of her father, a man whose whole life had been lived to the glory of God. Finally, there was the spiritual darkness in which she spent the last eighteen months of her life. There was her agonising last illness in which she had to suffer moment by moment, trusting in a God whose presence she could no longer feel, hoping against hope that there was indeed a heaven.

Thérèse is very close to our troubled modern age. There are many who do not believe in God, many who look for nothing beyond the grave. To all these, Thérèse brings a message of hope. It is the hope of one who has looked with love upon the figure of the Crucified and has understood the meaning of that life and death. It is the hope of one who sees Christ kneeling in the darkness, crying out in agony, mouthing the cry of black despair, "My god, my God, why?" It is the hope of one who has seen God incarnate wrestling with meaninglessness and rising triumphant from the grave where all his dreams lay buried. This is our God, who is with us on our journey from darkness to light. This is our God, who shares our sorrow and perplexity, who understands that often we are like children crying in the night.

Thérèse is a teacher who brings us close to God by reminding us that we are indeed children. Most of us are very ordinary; we cannot achieve great things. But to all of us is open the Little Way of childhood, the way of loving surrender and trust, the offering of each moment to our loving God. To all of us is open the way of creativity; we can all use the raw material of life, the joys and sorrows, to create the holy contentment which made Thérèse exclaim, "I like whatever God does." And all of us can rejoice, rather than lament, that at our death we shall appear before God with empty hands. Like Thérèse, we shall understand that, if we are empty of self-importance, aware of our powerlessness and poverty, God will fill our hands with his own riches.

Yes, Thérèse is the universal saint. She has plucked sanctity from the lofty heights and brought it within the reach of all souls of good will. She is the imitable saint, one who wished her Little Way to be accessible to a legion of little souls: ordinary people who seek to please God. She is a saint who first practised and then taught others her "new way to heaven." She is a doctor of the Church, not because she has brought a new teaching but because she has reminded us of an old teaching that many had forgotten: we are all called to be saints, we are all beloved children of a merciful God. This is the message of our great little doctor.

ENDNOTES

Chapter 2: Herald of Mercy
1. Ecclesiasticus 11:12-13

Chapter 3: A Little Way to Heaven
1. Proverbs 9:4
2. Isaiah 66:12 & 13
3. Last Conversations
4. *Story of a Soul*
5. Manuscript prayer of St Teresa
6. Romans 8:28
7. *Story of a Soul*, Epilogue
8. 11 Kings 5
9. Genesis ch.22
10. 1 Samuel 3
11. Jeremiah 1:10
12. Isaiah 64:6
13. 2 Peter 1:4
14. 1 Corinthians 3:21-23
15. 1 Corinthians 15:9 & 10
16. Luke 15:31
17. Julian of Norwich, Revelations
18. Last Conversations

Chapter 4: Thérèse Contemplative
1. Colossians 1:24
2. Guy Gaucher, O.C.D., *The Passion of Thérèse of Lisieux*

Chapter 5: Love and Thérèse
1. Last Conversations
2. *Story of a Soul*

Chapter 6: Creative Genius
1. 1 Corinthians 3:9

Chapter 7: Contentment
1. Philippians 4:11
2. Psalm 40:7 & 8
3. *Saint Teresa, Interior Castle*
4. *Where Silence is Praise*
5. Psalm18:19

Chapter 8: Thérèse and Friendship

1. *Story of a Soul*
2. *Prayers and Meditations of Saint Anselm*, Penguin Classics
3. Sister Mary of the Trinity. Pierre Descouvement. Les Editions du Cerf, Paris
4. Proverbs 27:6
5. Vie Thérèsienne, nos. 73 & 77
6. Letters
7. St Matthew 25:40

Chapter 9: Thérèse and Mary

1. Documents of Vatican II, *Lumen Gentium*, ch.IV
2. John 2:5
3. Poems
4. *Collected Works of Thérèse of Lisieux*
5. Galatians 4:19

Chapter 10: Duel with Darkness

1. Job 19:21
2. Isaiah 53:3
3. Isaiah 53:12
4. John 10:27
5. Job 13:15
6. Isaiah 53:12

Chapter 11: Empty Hands

1. Corinthians 8:9
2. Matthew 19:21
3. Last Conversations

Chapter 12: Universal Thérèse

1. Poems, Trans. Susan Leslie.
2. *St Thérèse By Those Who Knew Her*
3. Céline, R.P. Piat
4. Voltaire, Dialogues
5. *La Mort du Loup*, Translation Susan Leslie
6. Invictis

BIBLIOGRAPHY

Sources:
1. Knox, Ronald. *Autobiography of a Saint*, Thérèse of Lisieux, Trans. London, Harvill Press, 1958.
2. *The Collected Letters of St Thérèse of Lisieux*, London, Sheed & Ward, 1949.
3. *St Thérèse of Lisieux, Her Last Conversations*, I.C.S. Publications, Institute of Carmelite Studies, Washington, D.C., 1977.
4. *St Thérèse by those who knew her*, Veritas Publications, Dublin, 1975.

Studies:
1. Gaucher, Guy. *The Spiritual Journey of St Thérèse of Lisieux*, Darton, Longman & Todd, London, 1987.
2. O'Connor, Patricia. *In Search of Thérèse*, Darton, Longman & Todd, London, 1987.
3. Foley, Marc, O.C.D. *The love that keeps us sane*, Paulist Press, N.Jersey, 2000.